Brasseries & Bistros in Paris

 + 51 CLASSIC RECIPES

TECTUM
PUBLISHERS

© 2008   Tectum Publishers
         Godefriduskaai 22
         2000 Antwerp, Belgium
         info@tectum.be
         + 32 3 226 66 73
         www.tectum.be

ISBN: 978-90-76886-73-2
WD: 2008/9021/10
(52)

First published by
Editions Ereme
(French edition: EAN 9782915337471)

English translation: Victoria Mundy - Liberlab (Savigliano, Italy)

Brasseries & Bistros in Paris

Foreword
André Santini

Photography
Valentine Vermeil

Text
Matthieu Flory
Clémentine Forissier

TECTUM
PUBLISHERS

Foreword
André Santini

I never leave choosing a restaurant to chance. As Churchill said: "I am not difficult; I just like the best!". Because I grew up in a bistro (my father first opened one in the Barbès district, then its success helped him to buy a restaurant at the end of the Courbevoie bridge, *Le Petit Vatel*, which was soon renamed *Porto-Bar*), I truly have a taste for noisy bar environments, well-dressed tables and fine food.

The accelerated standardisation of food trends, in my opinion, therefore seems like an insult to - or worse, a crime against - good French taste, our culinary tradition and the pure chemistry which makes our bistros, brasseries and restaurants the last bastions of conviviality, seemingly a dirty word these days!

There is a simple explanation: people no longer talk to each other as they used to. Much more so than places of worship and sporting arenas, nowadays bistros encourage harmony between employees and their bosses, men and women (happily, more and more women are beginning to visit) and help to bridge the generation gap.

Actively seeking the pleasure of solitary dining is a vice which is disapproved of, morally speaking. Jean-Jacques Rousseau even wrote in his *Confessions*: "I only need pure pleasures. I love the pleasures of dining, for example, but I can only enjoy them with a friend. Alone, it is not possible: my mind starts to wander and I am not able to fully enjoy the simple experience of eating."

I regularly visit a brasserie opposite the town hall in Issy-les-Moulineaux, which for two years has been the hallowed "best bistro in... Paris". The atmosphere is authentic. The veal liver and ribsteak are incomparable. I rediscovered the atmosphere of my childhood there: the clink of glasses, the dessert blackboard, the haste of the waiters, the warm welcome of the smiling owner, bursts of laughter, shouts, and conversations which excite the neighbouring tables and which, due to the magic of the premises, soon become the sole topic of discussion.

This book lists the oldest bistros and restaurants in Paris. They are truly distinguishing features of the districts in which they are located: what would Montparnasse be without *La Closerie des Lilas*? Rue Royale without *Maxim's*? Or even the Champs-Élysées without *Fouquet's*? They are often the most beautiful and extraordinary pieces in the architectural puzzle of Paris. To dine there is not simply a gastronomic pleasure, but is also a feast for the eyes. How could anyone fail to notice the quality of the wood panels, the impeccably clean copperware, the transparency of the chandeliers on the third floor, or even the colourful plaster mouldings on the ceilings, the engraved glasses and the unusual bars with their two-tone marble surfaces?

But their appeal is also generated by other sources. They are genuine repositories of culture. It is often the case that these bistros and restaurants were once vibrant theatres for the movements which, between 1850 and 1930, assisted in the progression of ideas, arts and politics. Whether they hosted the most heated social debates or the most audacious artistic revolutions, they all tell us something about our history. Whether they were dining halls to which Classicists would withdraw, refuges for Modernists, dens for penniless artists or comfortable hideouts for powerful figures, they all have played a full part in the history of our culture. The effervescence of evenings prior to the execution of plots and the excitement generated by secret stolen moments can still be felt in these renowned establishments, where the echoes of celebratory evenings can still be heard. There is also something extremely moving about eating alongside the ghosts of famous customers.

This book is evidently of great worth: besides paying homage to our history, it is an ode to good taste. The recipes suggested for each of the establishments listed will help to convince you of this.

I must now stop my idle chit-chat and invite you to discover them for yourselves without further delay. Let's eat!

André SANTINI
Secretary of State
Mayor of Issy-les-Moulineaux

Index of bistros, brasseries and restaurants

1ˢᵗ District

2ⁿᵈ District

38, rue Montorgueil
75001 Paris
tel : 01.42.36.83.51

L'ESCARGOT MONTORGUEIL

A gilded snail sits proudly on the canopy of 38, rue Montorgueil. Stuffed with the shells of hundreds of small amber-coloured gastropods, the front window of the establishment speaks volumes about the atmosphere inside. The result of a partnership between its old owner, the wine merchant Bourreau, and the restaurateur Mignard, *L'Escargot d'Or* opened in 1874, using the motto: "Wine, snails and a restaurant".

Surrounded by Second Empire décor and overlooked by a panelled ceiling featuring arabesques, pearls and raised fruit dish designs, members of the Parisian bourgeoisie delighted in these small molluscs, which were served either simply cooked in garlic butter, in vol-au-vents or in a curry.

André Terrail, the owner of the prestigious *Tour d'Argent*, bought this renowned Les Halles stop-off point in 1919 and made his good friend Lespinas, who had previously been a cook for the king of Egypt, responsible for supervising the kitchen. The restaurant then acquired its fame:

on the first floor, accessed via a flight of spiral stairs, many politicians marked out their territory, while the cooking cherubs painted on the ceiling above the entrance (painted by Clarin for Sarah Bernhardt's dining room and purchased by André Terrail) invited the "Tout Paris" guide of the roaring twenties to slum it on the ground floor.

Welcoming and intimate, the restaurant has attracted a throng of celebrities from the worlds of art, literature and theatre throughout the XX century, for example Marcel Proust, Charlie Chaplin and Mistinguett, then later on Salvador Dali and Orson Welles.

When she took over the establishment in 1975, Kouikette Terrail, the daughter of André, restored the original décor: this included the black wood panelling, red seats and gilded mouldings, in addition to the diamond-patterned wooden shop front. Its original atmosphere has also remained intact and the snail still takes pride of place.

GUEUZAILLE SNAILS

Ingredients

(serves 4)

4 very large potatoes
36 Burgundy snails
20 g shallot
1 head of garlic
1/2 bunch parsley
400 g butter
80 g crème fraîche
Salt and pepper

Method

Cook the potatoes in their jackets.
Fry them in hot oil until the skin turns golden.
Chop the shallot, garlic and parsley very finely.
Mix with the crème fraîche and the softened butter.
Leave in the refrigerator for 15 minutes.
Use 2/3 of this mixture to fill the potatoes, which should have been cut open in the same way as boiled eggs and hollowed out using a small spoon.
Stuff each potato with 9 snails and place in the oven for 10 minutes.
Finish by pouring over the remaining sauce once it has been heated in a saucepan.
Garnish with a few sprigs of chervil and serve immediately.

17, rue du Beaujolais
75001 Paris
tel : 01.42.96.56.27

LE GRAND VÉFOUR

Le Grand Véfour is one of the extremely rare Parisian venues to have retained all the features of its XVIII century décor.

The establishment, which opened in rue du Beaujolais in 1784, was originally called *Le Café des Chartres*. It was the result of a major reorganisation programme for the Palais Royal gardens, a project undertaken by the owner at that time, Philippe of Orleans, the Duke of Chartres, who decided to divide part of his land into several plots in order to pay off his debts. This led to the construction of rues de Montpensier, Valois and Beaujolais. It is said that the gardens, which the police were prohibited from entering at that time, provided the setting for all kinds of extravagance and excess: extremely scantily-clad women, or even Joséphine de Beauharnais, could be seen there, enjoying the company of the opposite sex.

Le Café des Chartres, which occupies the entire width of the Joinville peristyle, was taken over in 1820 by Jean Véfour, who named it after himself. It then became a leading establishment in Parisian gastronomy and Thiers,

Mac-Mahon, Victor Hugo, Lamartine, Georges Sand, Chopin and many others came to meet here.

Le Grand Véfour closed in 1905 and was then brought back to life in 1948; from then on it was a popular venue for artists and writers such as Cocteau (who designed the menu art), Colette, Sacha Guitry, Jean-Paul Sartre and Simone de Beauvoir...

After it was taken over by the *Taittinger* group in the early 1980s, the restaurant, under the direction of Guy Martin, once again became a significant destination on the gastronomic map. Wood panelling carved into Louis XVI garlands is still on display here, while the walls are hung with rare and beautiful painted toiles inspired by frescoes from Pompeii; these are fixed in place under a sheet of glass and separated by large mirrors. The aim of the toiles was probably to awaken the appetite of guests, as they depict tasty vegetables, game and fish, as well as women carrying baskets of flowers. On the ceiling, stucco roses and garlands surround odes to womankind, in the style of XVIII century Italian ceilings.

JERUSALEM ARTICHOKES A LA DARPHIN

Ingredients

(serves 4)

600 g Jerusalem artichokes
4 dried figs
150 g butter
1 tablespoon potato flour
Salt, freshly ground pepper
Fleur de sel (Brittany salt)

Method

Clarify the butter: melt the butter over a low heat until it becomes clear and a whitish residue is deposited on the base of the saucepan. Remove the pan from the heat and use a small ladle or a spoon to collect the clear part. Peel the Jerusalem artichokes. Grate them into a fine julienne and roll them in the clarified butter, then the potato flour. Add salt and pepper.
Cut the figs into 5 or 6 slices.
Take 4 non-stick frying pans with a diameter of 12 cm. Use half the Jerusalem artichokes to line the bottom of each pan. Next, create a layer of figs, then cover with the rest of the Jerusalem artichokes.
Place the pans over a low heat and cook for 10 minutes, until the vegetables begin to colour, then turn using a spatula and cook the other side for a further 10 minutes.
Drain on kitchen paper and serve with a few grains of the fleur de sel.

1, Place du Châtelet
75001 Paris
tel : 01.42.36.74.03

LE ZIMMER

At the turn of the century, Monsieur Zimmer created one of the most beautiful brasseries in Paris, right next door to the Châtelet theatre, for which it became an antechamber of sorts.

Like many of his fellow Alsatians (Bofinger, Floderer, Zeyer, Wepler), Zimmer arrived in Paris soon after the war in 1870, with his native Alsace packed away in his luggage. The "beer and stucco" equation was a recipe for success at that time, so in 1896 Zimmer opened one of the most flamboyant brasseries in Paris. Spread over four floors, it was located right next to the Châtelet theatre; the two establishments were linked via an amazing network of doors on the ground floor and the other levels.

This was all that was needed to make the venue a retreat for any Parisians associated with the Arts. Musicians, writers, painters and actors used to meet in the large restaurant, which could hold up to one hundred and fifty guests, or in the small private rooms on the other floors.

At that time, guests would have crossed paths with Jules Verne, gracefully greeting Sarah Bernhardt and her hordes of admirers. Mahler, Debussy and Strauss would go there to discuss Wagner and dodecaphony. Dancing and the Ballets Russes were also well represented, with Nijinski and Diaghilev "strutting about" under the amused gaze of Picasso or Apollinaire. The rush was such that a real mini-army - consisting of huntsmen, window cleaners, soft drinks salesmen, cutlery specialists, cellar men and even firemen - was needed to respond to the many requirements of this distinguished crowd.

It had been quite a journey from the time when *Le Courrier Français* had to reassure Parisians of the patriotism of the recently-opened establishment, which was struggling to attract customers... During the Second World War, the "Honneur de la Police" resistance network held a number of meetings in the huge basements underneath the premises, enabling several lucky families to escape the anti-Semitic raids which were taking place at that time.

A few years ago, the owners asked the famous Parisian interior designer Jacques Garcia to restore a little glamour to the sluggish establishment. It was he who designed the current layout of the premises, infusing it with welcoming modernity after successfully reviving the mouldings, gilding and painted ceilings inside it.

Continuing its long tradition, *Le Zimmer* still organises literary events, which are held in its large room.

MONKFISH WITH SWEET PEPPERS AND TAPENADE

Ingredients

(serves 4)

8 monkfish portions, each
weighing approximately 80 g
6 tablespoons single cream
30 g tapenade
2 green peppers, 2 red peppers
and 2 yellow peppers,
deseeded and skins removed
4 tablespoons olive oil
Fleur de sel, salt and pepper

Method

In a saucepan, bring the cream to the boil, add the tapenade, mix well and stop just before it begins boiling again. Season, remove from the heat and set aside.

Cut the peppers into strips and heat them in a casserole dish, with the olive oil. Season and cook for 5 minutes over a low heat, stirring and making sure they remain crisp. Set aside.

Cut the monkfish into 2 cm slices and cook in a very hot pan with some olive oil for 2-3 minutes on each side, so the slices are opaque right to the very centre. Season and set aside.

When assembling the dish, reheat the sauce over a low heat for 2 minutes, then divide the peppers between the plates, place the monkfish medallions on top and pour over the sauce.

32, rue Saint-Marc
75002 Paris
tel : 01.42.96.65.04

AUX LYONNAIS

Just a few steps from the Opéra Comique, a welcoming painted wooden facade conceals a Lyonnais-style bistro which looks as if it has come straight out of the last century.

Shortly after the Salle Favart was destroyed by the famous fire of 1887, a small café opened for business at number 32, rue Saint-Marc. The labourers working on the reconstruction of the Opéra went there on their breaks and, when the project was completed in 1898, were replaced by drivers who patiently waited for their employers as they attended concerts in the neighbouring establishment.

It was only in 1955 that Monsieur Viollet took over the bistro, giving it the name we recognise today and transforming it into a real temple of Lyonnais cooking. Since then, fritons, tabliers de sapeur, poulardes demi-deuil and pike quenelles in Nantua sauce have been served in great quantities to a Parisian clientele charmed as much by the generous portions on offer as by the warm and welcoming décor.

This small bistro is certainly not lacking in the charm department: the interior design scheme and the front of the premises date back to the opening of the café and yet never appear outdated. Cream wood panelling decorated with floral garlands cover the walls, while métro-style earthenware tiles cover the lower part of the building. The décor also includes several pieces by Jean-Claude Novaro, a renowned glassworker from Biot, which are reflected in bevelled mirrors on both floors.

The "nouvelle cuisine" which emerged in the 1970s meant the bistro sank progressively further into oblivion, until its fortunes were revived in 2002 by Alain Ducasse and Thierry de la Brosse, the owner of *L'Ami Louis*. Under their guidance, the tiles were restored and the ground floor level updated with a large tin and zinc-plated wooden bar, on top of which sits an old piston coffee machine.

Guests are once again able to sit at patinated oak tables and sample some of the great classic dishes in Lyonnais cuisine.

BRESSE CHICKEN

deglaced with aged wine and vinegar

Ingredients

(serves 4)

1 Bresse chicken weighing
approximately 1.5 kg (giblets
removed)
125 g butter
100 ml aged wine vinegar
200 ml Alsatian chicken stock
100 ml chicken stock
500 ml single cream
Salt, freshly ground pepper

Method

Cut the chicken into 4 large pieces. Use a sauté pan
to brown all sides in the butter for a few minutes.
Season, then deglaze the pan using the aged wine
vinegar. Next, add the Alsatian chicken stock.
Place everything in a casserole dish and cook for
approximately 20-25 minutes, in an oven preheated
to 100°C. Make sure it is cooked, then set the
pieces of chicken aside.
Reduce the cooking juices until they have almost
evaporated, then add the single cream and the
chicken stock. Reduce again, until the sauce has
thickened considerably.
Pour the sauce over the pieces of chicken.

Serve, if desired, with a hot foie blond terrine.

Place Gaillon
75002 Paris
tel : 01.47.42.63.22

LA FONTAINE GAILLON

In 2003, two famous French film stars opened this charming establishment in a prestigious and distinctive hotel on the Place Gaillon, just a few steps from the Opéra.

In 1672, Mr Nicolas Frémont, an officer at the Palais Royal, asked Jules Hardouin-Mansart, the famous architect who designed part of the Palace of Versailles, to assist in the construction of his unique hotel next to the Gaillon gate, which at that time marked the boundary of Louis XIV's Paris. His son-in-law the Duke of Lorge, whose eldest daughter would later marry the Duke of Saint-Simon, demolished the gate a few years later in order to extend his residence. In 1707, the first fountain, constructed by Jean de Beausire and named after Louis the Great, appeared at the front of the hotel. Visconti, the creator of Emperor Napoleon I's tomb, would restore it a century later to reflect a more modern style. The building passed through the hands of several distinguished owners, such as Princess Bourbon-Conti, the Duke of Richelieu and a Spanish Ambassador, before being trans-formed into a restaurant in the second half of the XX century.

The establishment, called *Pierre à la fontaine Gaillon*, was taken over four years ago by Gérard Depardieu and Carole Bouquet, who renovated the entire building while preserving several original features. The Antin fountain still adorns the beautiful façade, and impressive stone fireplaces can still be found inside the rooms.

The new owners, who are extremely interested in art, have filled the spaces inside the premises with several pieces: a small room on the first floor is dedicated to Jean Cocteau, while lithographs by André Masson, texts by René Char and various, more contemporary works are on display in the four other special rooms, or in the rooms on the ground floor.

Guests can savour the rich regional cuisine of chef Laurent Audiot in this setting, which swings between classicism and modernity, or on the shady terrace.

SPIT-ROAST SUCKLING PIG

stuffed with herbs

Ingredients

(serves 4)

1 small suckling pig, aged 5
weeks maximum
100 g slightly salted butter
1 large bunch flat-leaf parsley
1 bunch tarragon
1 bunch chives
1 bunch chervil
3 sprigs thyme
2 bay leaves
1 pinch Esplette chilli
Salt and pepper
1 tablespoon Cognac

Method

Wash the herbs and dry them using kitchen paper, chop roughly; break up the thyme and bay leaves. Prepare the stuffing: melt the butter in a saucepan, add all the herbs and the liver of the suckling pig. Add salt and pepper. Add a tablespoon of Cognac, if required, and the Esplette chilli. Mix well until a good stuffing has formed. Fill the cavity of the pig with this stuffing, close it up, stitch together the stomach walls with string and close up all the orifices.

Stick the pig on a spit or a large roaster and fix the trotters against the body using small wooden skewers. Use the spit to turn the pig slowly over very hot embers and pour hot salted water over it every so often during the cooking process. Cook for approximately 30 minutes per pound.

When the pig is just cooked through, stop cooking and remove it from the spit. Cut it into generous slices and serve with the stuffing inside. Spoon some of the cooking juices over the slices of meat.

40, rue Notre-Dame des Victoires
75002 Paris
tel 01 43 54 12 12

GALLOPIN

The first Anglo-American bar in Paris... Gustave Gallopin, a successful beer seller, slowly came round to this idea during a visit to New York at the turn of the XIX century.

It all began in 1876, when Gallopin signed the lease for a shop at number 40, rue Notre-Dame-des-Victoires, opposite the Palais Brongniart. The sale of beer progressed well; Gallopin served many stock exchange clerks and figures from the theatre industry. He quickly became successful, extending and restoring the two shops next to number 40. Meeting and marrying a wealthy English woman led to him travelling frequently, discovering different lifestyles from across the Channel and the Atlantic. Gallopin was seduced by this new type of style, as "exotic" as it was welcoming, and began to catch glimpses of the commercial success such an adventure could bring in terms of the Parisian population. This would allow people to drink while reconsidering their surroundings, letting them travel and letting them dream...

Number 40, rue Notre-Dame-des-Victoires would come to symbolise the successful marriage of Victorian England, *fin de siècle* New York and the Hausmannian Paris of the Stock Exchange: Gallopin created *Le Grand Bar* there, importing an impressive revolving door from New York (which has since been removed for safety reasons), while the bar and the Victorian wood decoration, made using beautiful Cuban

mahogany, were sent from London. The entire simple, impressive and solid setting was rhythmically punctuated by gilded copperware studded horizontally along the large room, while the silver-plated metal beer tankards were happily lined up behind the bar (a new unit of measurement, the gallopin, had been specially invented by the owner in order to create a 250 ml "French pint"). The mahogany panelling was enhanced by gilded Ionic pillars and the walls were adorned with large basket-handle arched mirrors. Continuing with his plans for expansion a few years later, Gustave Gallopin rented part of the inner courtyard to celebrate the new century, commissioning a stained-glass window and an elegant Art Nouveau glass roof.

The establishment changed hands in 1906, with Camille Aymonier taking charge and moving towards further expansion: employers could be found at the *Grand Bar*, while agents took great delight in the *Petit Bar* and assistants and clerks enjoyed themselves in number 42.

Four families then took over in succession, but it would be 1997 before Gallopin was entirely restored by Monsieur and Madame Alexandre, the current owners of the premises. Since then, figures from the theatre industry, actors and journalists have been coming here to enjoy true brasserie-style cuisine washed down with fine champagnes...

CRÊPES "ALEXANDRE"

Ingredients

(serves 1)

5 g sugar
1 knob of butter
1 orange
1 lemon
3 crêpes
20 ml Grand Marnier rouge
20 ml Cointreau

Method

Steep the orange and lemon peel in the Cointreau and Grand Marnier rouge for 24 hours.

Heat the sugar in a frying pan and tip in the orange and lemon zest, with none of the pith still attached.

Cut an orange in two and squeeze it directly into the pan.

Squeeze half of the lemon and loosen the mixture of ingredients in the pan, beating it together with the lemon juice using the end of a fork.

Bring to the boil and leave to reduce for 10 seconds.

Soak the crêpes in this mixture and fold them into triangles, then add both alcohols.

Flambé while sprinkling over the sugar, in order to caramelise the crêpes.

Arrange the crêpes on a warmed plate, opening them up slightly. Pour over the sauce until the crêpes are fully covered.

4, rue Vivienne
75002 Paris
tel : 01.42.86.87.88

LE GRAND COLBERT

Constructed on the site of an old, distinctive building owned by the famous minister who served Louis XIV, renowned for his fine palace, this elegant brasserie has remained lively through the ages, feeding theatrical and literary Paris... as well as the old French National Library, which owns the premises. The Library was also behind the 1985 restoration project which allowed the establishment to regain its former glory.

The majestic spaces - with high ceilings and amazing depth - immediately grab your attention, and are enhanced with a long, beautiful antique wood bar featuring a beautiful belt of gilded copper.

Hand-painted frescoes cover the walls, mixing floral patterns and medallions with a celebration of the culinary arts, in the manner of the colourful interior decoration styles dating back to the middle of the last century.

The most striking decorative element is undoubtedly the collection of beautiful and colourful mosaics on the floor, created by G. Fachina, which is identical to the collection on the floor of the Vivienne Gallery, the other side of the Library. Large golden yellow spirals coil around black circle arcs, at the centre of which small yellow, white and red cubes surround proud black stars. This merry-go-round of small squares and colours brings an extra touch of excitement to the premises, where huge dark wood standard lamps cast their soft yellowish-red light over colourful exotic vegetation.

Somewhere between hubbub and joviality, this stunning space remains a favourite destination for various figures from the worlds of theatre, fashion and cinema, who flock here to enjoy traditional cuisine.

ENGLISH-STYLE PAN-FRIED VEAL LIVER

Ingredients

(serves 4)

4 slices veal liver
4 thin slices bacon
1 tablespoon aged wine vinegar
1 small bunch flat-leaf parsley
20 g butter
Salt, freshly ground pepper

Method

Wash the parsley, remove the stalks and chop it.
Grill the slices of bacon in a very hot frying pan without any oil until crisp, then set aside and keep warm.
Remove any excess fat from the pan, then add the butter and wait until it begins to bubble. Add the liver slices and fry for 3 minutes on each side. Set aside and keep warm, discarding the excess fat produced by cooking. Deglaze the frying pan with the vinegar. Add salt and pepper.
Arrange the dish: lay the liver slices on plates, add the cooked bacon and drizzle with the vinegar.

3rd District

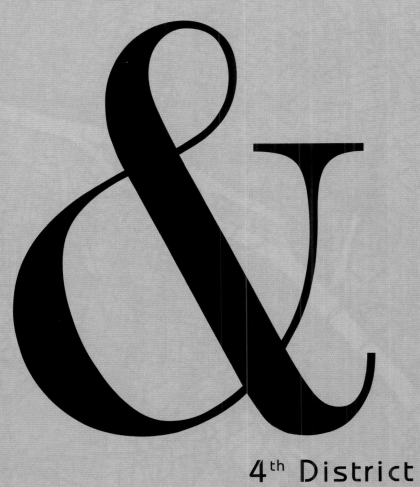

4th District

32, rue Vertbois
75002 Paris
tel : 01.48.87.77.48

L'AMI LOUIS

Behind the red and white checked curtains in the window, a few American stars and wealthy industrialists sit at the tables in a small, rustic and simple room known as *L'Ami Louis*.

Yet Louis Pedebosque started out in quite a simple manner. "Ami Louis", from the Landes, set up his restaurant in number 32, rue Vertbois and seven years later joined forces with Antoine Magnin, whose know-how brought the establishment great success, attracting a clientele which at times was so varied that it was almost comical.

Situated near the École Centrale and the Conservatoire des Arts et Métiers (a respected art and technology school), the establishment was a popular meeting place for students such as Marcel Dassault. Sacha Guitry, Yvonne Printemps and Pierre Brasseur would go there to relax after performances in the theatres along the Grands Boulevards, while the rich patrons of local brothels enjoyed delicious intervals there...

The Second World War paradoxically contributed to raising the profile of *L'Ami Louis* overseas. Used as an American army base during the conflict, the Conservatoire des Arts et Métiers led many soldiers to frequent the establishment. One of them, who later became chief editor of a leading American newspaper, wrote several articles about the restaurant on his return. Americans visiting Paris have been eager to stop there ever since.

Bill Clinton and Jacques Chirac had dinner at this restaurant during an official visit. This is, however, linked to another story: Francis Ford Coppola, a loyal customer of *L'Ami Louis*, one day asked the entire team to cook for his friends while he was on holiday in France. The group then became acquainted with several personalities, including a few members of the Clinton family, who were immediately won over by the quality and simplicity of the food.

Antoine Magnin died, virtually whilst cooking, in 1986, but his presence is still strongly felt in the restaurant: two photographs taken by Milos Forman - one of the restaurant's long-standing regulars - of the boss in a cook's uniform, with his long white beard and laughing eyes, still hang on the wall today.

The atmosphere of *L'Ami Louis*, which has since been taken over by an old partner, has not changed. The décor has remained the same since it was opened: the worn red hexagonal floor tiles, walls and aged mirrors, the marble tables and even the copper pans dating back to 1845 are still in use today. The whole roasted Bresse guinea fowl and the enormous entrecôtes are still cooked in the wood-burning oven. Only the wine cellar has been extended; space simply had to be found for the restaurant's 19,000 bottles...

OVEN-ROASTED RIBSTEAK AND CEPS

Ingredients

(serves 2)

800 g ribsteak
2 tablespoons goose fat
1 kg ceps
1 clove garlic
Coarse salt
Guérande salt
Pepper
1/2 bunch parsley
1/2 bunch basil
30 g butter

Method

Leave the ribsteak at room temperature for 1 hour. Spread a little goose fat and coarse salt over it, then grill for a few minutes over a wood fire. Next, leave it in a wood-burning oven for 20 minutes (or approximately 40 minutes in a traditional oven at 200°C).

Meanwhile, rinse the ceps under running water and leave them to dry on a cloth for 20 minutes.

Put a little oil on a plate and add the whole ceps, without chopping them. Place them in the wood-burning oven for approximately 40 minutes (or in a traditional oven for a good hour), so that they release their juices. Next, add the garlic after crushing it in the palm of your hand, with a little butter.

At the last minute, add the snipped parsley and basil and grind a generous amount of pepper over the food using a pepper mill.

49, rue Volta
75003 Paris
tel : 01.48.87.88.24

ANAHI

Any passer-by who is not familiar with *Anahi* will probably walk right past number 28 rue Volta, one of the most extraordinary - and run-down - shop fronts in Paris. However, if by chance this passer-by were to walk through the door, he would certainly be won over by the unusual charm found within this one-time butcher's shop, now a temple of Hispanic gastronomy.

The adventure began in 1928, in a small side street in the Sentier district. A pork butcher decided to set up his business there, just a few steps from the Place de la République. Fascinated by the Art Deco movement, he redecorated the entire ground floor of the building. Covering the walls of his business premises in white checks, he also asked a certain Monsieur Camus, who some claim could have been the brother of the writer Albert, to create a false ceiling featuring geometric patterns, which to this day remains one of the only examples of its kind in France (the majority of these features were implemented during the Art Nouveau movement). To draw attention to the new function of the premises, the new owner commissioned stained-glass windows with an animal theme, inviting passers-by to come and sample the poultry and game on offer inside the shop. These win-

dows can still be seen today.

Immediately following the war, the establishment was purchased by a textile merchant and became a jeans warehouse, before being transformed into a Slavic restaurant. In the 1970s, an Argentine and a Chilean moved into the premises, then in 1985 the property was taken over by three sisters, two of whom still own it today. They renamed it *Anahi*, after an ill-fated Bolivian princess.

These most recent owners chose to leave everything as they found it, including the shop front, where the marble slabs dating back to 1930 have become progressively weathered due to the incessant comings and goings of the lorries in the Sentier district.
Besides a few rows of bottles, the only decoration is provided by three black and white photographs hung on the walls and a cactus positioned behind one of the windows.

This unusual setting, combined with the simple yet tasty Spanish and South American-inspired cuisine, fascinates artists and film-makers alike, even enchanting the world of fashion on the occasions when it hosts after-show gatherings.

MANCHAMANTELES (TABLECLOTH-STAINING STEW)

Ingredients

(serves 4)

1 kg diced pork shoulder
2 tablespoons mole sauce
(at Israël, Paris)
3 cloves garlic, minced
1 Pasilla chilli
1 Cascabel chilli
1 Mulato chilli
1 handful oregano
10 - 12 dried apricots
1 handful prunes
2 courgettes
2 green apples
Peanut oil

Method

In a casserole dish, heat the peanut oil and fry the garlic. Add the meat and brown it for 5 minutes.
Next, add a handful of oregano and cook over a high heat. After another 5 minutes, add the mole sauce, followed by the 3 chopped and deseeded chillies. Add water so that the level is halfway up the side of the dish, then leave to cook over a low heat for approximately 1 hour. Add the dried apricots half-way through, then the prunes 5 minutes later. Add a little more water if necessary. Add the two courgettes, sliced into rounds, 5 to 10 minutes before the end.
Once the courgettes are cooked, remove the dish from the heat and add the 2 green apples, cut into thick slices. Serve.

32, rue du Picardie
75003 Paris
tel : 01.44.54.20.60

GUILLAUME

At the beginning of the last century, a large goldsmith's workshop designed by the *Ateliers Eiffel* opened in rue de Picardie, a few minutes' walk from the Carreau du Temple. It experienced varying fortunes before being taken over by Guillaume, who turned it into a restaurant in 2005.

The new owner wanted to preserve the industrial identity of the premises and put its incredible rooms to good use. There are three levels in this 400 m² space, split into a ground floor and two mezzanines underneath the immense glass roof covering the structure. Work had to be carried out on the site in order to give the premises the warm and insular feel which is part of its appeal today. All elements dating back to the Eiffel era (such as girders and metal) were preserved, while the walls were soundproofed and repainted. All decorative tasks were supervised carefully: Guillaume spent many hours searching second-hand shops for objects which would fit in with this unusual setting. This is how he came across the white metal lampshades suspended above the central table, as well as a lot of the furniture in the restaurant.

The welcoming and pleasant atmosphere of *Guillaume* is not simply a concept, but the result of a project led by the owner himself, who enlisted the help of family and friends when searching for the pieces of art on display throughout the restaurant. A few particularly memorable examples of this are as follows: his mother provided the sleeves from old jazz albums so that they could be hung on the wall, and a stage designer friend of his, Nicolas Henry, designed the patchwork decoration hanging over the large table. This artist also created the stunning "piano explosion", reminiscent of work by Arman, which is suspended under the glass roof. It is plain to see that Guillaume has created an artistic laboratory within this industrial setting, as he regularly organises exhibitions in addition to offering elegant cuisine inspired by countries all over the world. The involvement of the owner and his circle of family and friends gives this restaurant true character and sincere warmth, which integrates amazingly well into this extraordinary setting.

RUM BABA

with ginger and pineapple jam, served with vanilla ice cream

Ingredients

(serves 4)

4 rum babas
Rum
250 ml single cream
3 g vanilla powder
1 Victoria pineapple
500 ml water
250 g sugar
20 g ginger

Method

Peel and dice the pineapple finely, then place it in a saucepan with the water, sugar and chopped ginger. Leave to cook over a low heat, until the liquid becomes a jam.

Put the cream and vanilla in a container, whip to make a Chantilly and add the icing sugar while whisking vigorously.

Spoon the candied pineapple and its syrup onto a deep plate and place the rum baba on top, then carefully place two spoonfuls of the Chantilly cream in the middle. Garnish with a pineapple leaf.

BENOÎT

"Always keep your ambitions realistic, without turning into a gourmand, and you will never lose your soul...". The grandson of this family restaurant's founder made this wise motto his own, thus preserving the spirit of this warm and welcoming establishment for almost thirty years.

When 18-year old Benoît Matray first arrived in Paris in 1904, the thought of entering the restaurant trade had not even crossed the young butcher's mind; he was simply visiting an uncle who ran a restaurant in the Les Halles district. He immediately fell in love with Paris and its atmosphere. The young Benoît abandoned his hometown of Lyon to sharpen his knives in the family restaurant and learn the trade, which he did until 1912, when he had saved enough money to open his own business just a short walk away.

From then on, number 20, rue Saint-Martin, with its straightforward and good-humoured atmosphere, opened at lunchtimes and in the evenings, to welcome part of the crowd moving through the impressive Les Halles market area. Butchers, specialist pork butchers, market gardeners and all types of other customers gathered at

Benoît, to sample cuisine based on kidney, tripe, tongue and heart. The portions were generous, the atmosphere pleasant and the business - and its reputation - prospered. In fact, it was so successful that in 1932 the restaurant received honours in the *Guide Escoffier*. A great number of journalists and politicians went there regularly, enjoying real complicity with the owner, who by that time weighed almost 150 kilos (just over 23 st 8 lbs).

His grandson took up the torch in 1968 and was awarded a *Michelin* star in 1970, while trying his best to preserve the good-humoured bourgeois atmosphere: the main room is still accessed through a beautiful dark wood double swing-door. In this room, old posters displaying old-fashioned humour decorate cream walls which have been subtly enhanced with several veins of imitation marble; the spaces within the room are punctuated and made more intimate through the interplay between copper-ware and mirrors. The special, discreet room on the first floor, which boasts a beautiful painted ceiling, old por-traits and a large table, can hold up to a dozen customers who require a warm welcome with a greater sense of intimacy...

JELLIED SKATE LOAF

Ingredients

(serves 8)

5 kg raw skate (1.7 kg
once filleted)
15 gelatine leaves
20 fresh mint leaves
300 g fresh tomatoes
50 g chopped shallots
5 fresh spinach leaves, cut into
strips

For the court-bouillon:
750 g onions
3 cloves garlic
750 g carrots
1 bouquet garni
2 bottles dry white wine
1/4 litre vinegar

Method

Boil and flambé the white wine. Add the diced carrot, the sliced onion, the garlic and the bouquet garni. Cover and simmer gently. Add the vinegar, the deseeded tomatoes and some salt and pepper. Reduce until you are left with 1.25 litres of stock. Add the gelatine and the 20 mint leaves.

Poach the filleted skate without boiling it. Assemble the skate loaf in a mould, alternating layers of skate with layers of the vegetables used to make the court-bouillon. Pour over the court-bouillon liquid until everything is covered.

Leave to cool; the skate loaf will become jellified. Serve in quarters, garnished with a chopped shallot, mint leaf and spinach-spiked vinaigrette.

5-7, rue de la Bastille
75004 Paris
tel : 01.42.72.87.82

BOFINGER

Perhaps one of the first great Alsatian brasseries to appear in Paris, *Bofinger* is surely the most awe-inspiring and successful example. Yet there was nothing luxurious about the small establishment when it was founded by Frédéric Bofinger in 1864: it sold pork products and sauerkraut, accompanied with beer served from the barrel - a great novelty at the time - in a welcoming but simple setting, inspired by the Alsatian weinstubs. The concept took off quickly and from then on, number 5, rue de la Bastille became one of the most popular places to visit in the capital.

The business grew significantly thanks to Albert Bruneau, the son-in-law of its founder, who took the reins in 1906, taking over the main room and designing a stage. It was not until after the First World War, in 1919, that the large-scale work (which gave *Bofinger* its current layout) started: the architect Lagay and the interior designer Mitgen threw themselves into the creation of a large dome featuring a floral pattern, while part of the first floor, which these days is called the "Room of the five continents", was refurbished. Since then, customers have crowded into the establishment to dine under the lights which cast their enchanting light over the tall bunches of blue flowers as they soar up the sky blue dome, their pro-

gress only halted by a border of grapes, leaves and various other flowers.

The décor across the rest of the ground floor and the stage is like a great shout of love - where the melody has been co-signed by the greatest Alsatian names - to the lost region: as the colonial exhibition of 1933 drew near, the great Hansi temporarily abandoned his caricatures and illustrated books to create the frescoes in the main room on the first floor, which have since been backed. Kugelhopf, pretzels, storks and ladybirds have also been at home on the patinated wood walls of the famous establishment since then.

Although *Bofinger* brings true happiness to exiled Alsatians, the premises has become an obligatory crossing point for all politicians, who find themselves sitting next to everyone perceived as actors and artists in Paris. This is so much the case that it would be futile to try and take a census of its illustrious occupants, who come from all four corners of the globe. There are rumours that certain governments may have fallen there after the sauerkraut had been washed down rather too effectively, and that great, idyllic love stories began there...

KUGELHOPF FRENCH TOAST
quetsche plum compote and caramel ice cream

Ingredients

(serves 4)

1 Kugelhopf weighing 500 g (or a fruited brioche), left to go stale
200 g Quetsche plums in syrup
250 ml caramel ice cream
250 ml custard
1 bunch fresh mint
4 eggs
700 ml milk
100 g sugar
100 g butter
1 glass Marc de Gewurztraminer brandy

Method

Cut the Kugelhopf into thick slices.
Mix the eggs and the sugar and add the milk, stirring everything together (all these ingredients should be cold). Dip the slices in this mixture and fry them in the butter. Sauté the Quetsche plums with the Marc de Gewurztraminer brandy, sprinkle over the sugar and flambé them using a clear spirit made of distilled fruit wine.
When dessert is served, pour the custard onto the base of each plate. Mould the Quetsche plums into a quenelle. Arrange the Kugelhopf slices in a fan shape and place a scoop of caramel ice cream next to the Questche plums. Garnish with 3 mint leaves.

53 bis, rue des Francs-Bourgeois
75004 Paris
tel : 01.42.74.54.17

LE DÔME DU MARAIS

Behind the very classic façade of 53 bis, rue des Francs-Bourgeois lies a completely unexpected style of décor. At the end of a stone corridor, a wide, "circus-red" stained-glass door opens onto a bright paved courtyard dotted with greenery and covered with a glass roof. It also provides access to an immense circular tower crowned with an engraved glass dome.

Bought at the end of the XVIII century, when the pawn shops recently introduced into France by Louis XVI were experiencing great success, this building in the old rue de Paradis was renovated by the architect Charles-François Viel de Saint-Maux. Inspired by the corn exchange, the commodities exchange and the Rotonde de la Villette, the main room - a circular tower topped with a hard limestone and semi-precious stone dome, with an openwork design at the centre - was intended as a real temple for the exchange industry.

After this, a metal dome provided the finishing touch of the structure for a while, until it was replaced once more during the Eiffel era, this time with an engraved glass version. The limited size of the premises led to the end of trading for this pawn shop in 1930, and the tower was then left abandoned, disused and neglected.

Transformed into a restaurant in 1981, the whole building was restored under the leadership of Roger Bénévant, who had envisaged a decoration scheme created by one of Viollet-le-Duc's pupils on his return from a trip to Pompeii: the foundations and mouldings of the dome were painted red, while subtly aged gold leaf-gilded decorations adorned the edges of the circular gallery and the alcoves within the building. All the decorative elements added were carefully researched in order to create a geometric structure based on the golden ratio; the central sculpture was the pivotal point around which this new design revolved.

When he arrived in 1998, Pierre Lecoutre - with the blessing of Roger Bénévant - decided to revive the colours used inside the premises, now renamed *Le Dôme du Marais*, and turned the adjoining courtyard into a second room by building a glass roof over it. Regulars and new guests alike are now able to dine in broad daylight or by the light of the moon in winter, just as they would in the summer months.

PEACHES IN CARPENTRAS LIME BLOSSOM SYRUP

with currant sorbet

Ingredients

(serves 10)

3 kg white peaches
50 g lime blossom tea
1/4 vanilla pod
Zest of 2 lemons
200 g sugar
2 l water
6 oranges
1 kg currant purée
250 g icing sugar

Method

Make incisions in the white peaches and blanch for 12 seconds; peel and cut into quarters.
To make the syrup, boil the water, sugar, lemon zest, vanilla and the juice from the oranges. When the mixture boils, add the lime blossom tea and leave to infuse for 20 minutes. Sieve the mixture, cook the peaches in their syrup over a low heat for 5 minutes and set aside in a cool place.
To make the sorbet, mix the currant purée and icing sugar together.
Crystallise the lime blossom tea leaves.
Lay 6 peach quarters in each deep plate and pour over the cooking juices. Place three sprigs of currants on the side, a scoop of sorbet in the middle and lay a few of the crystallised lime blossom tea leaves on top.

19, rue Beaubourg
75004 Paris
tel : 01.44.78.47.99

GEORGES

Georges, which is situated at the top of the Pompidou Centre and enjoys one of the most beautiful views in Paris, is one of the most exciting architectural creations of the last ten years.

The decision to open a restaurant at the top of the National Modern Art Museum was taken while restoration work was being carried out at the Pompidou Centre (the project was completed in 2000). The great challenge was the introduction of a new style of architecture within the original creation by Renzo Piano and Richard Rogers. The Costes brothers, who purchased the concession, asked the firm Jakob and MacFarlane to create an establishment which would blend into this specific style of architecture without distorting it, but which would also retain the personality of the features within it.

The architectural duo were keen to preserve the unusual space of the Beaubourg while expressing their own style. Inside the space - and without even touching the walls -

they developed a range of free-form aluminium structures shooting up from the floor, calling to mind the living bodies spreading throughout the building. The structures also offer their own response to the famous pipes running along the ceilings and installed around the outside of the building. The colour scheme (blue, red, yellow and green, representing air, fluids, electricity ducts and traffic movement) originally devised by the architects who designed the Centre was continued inside the structure by Jakob and MacFarlane.

Scattered amongst and alongside these strange features, tables and chairs with a pure, linear design receive guests in the large room or on the terrace and contrast beautifully with the curves inside the restaurant. Guests in this sophisticated environment can sample brasserie cuisine spiced up with several Asian dishes, while contemplating the crowds gathering at the foot of the Pompidou Centre or Notre Dame cathedral.

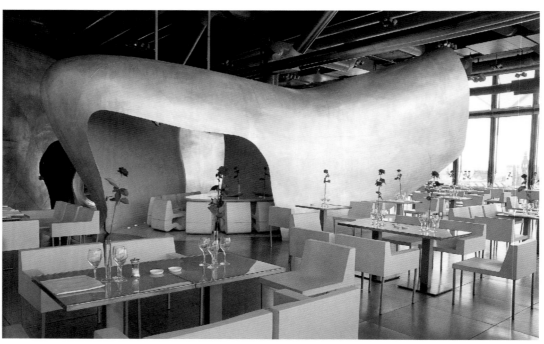

THE CRYING TIGER

Ingredients

(serves 4)

4 sirloin steaks, each weighing
200 g
For the marinade: 3 tablespoons
oyster sauce
1 tablespoon soy sauce
1 tablespoon spicy shrimp paste
1 tablespoon Cognac
1 tablespoon well-crushed garlic
3 tablespoons groundnut oil
1 teaspoon ground black pepper
For the sauce: 3 tablespoons
lime juice
1 teaspoon fish sauce
1 teaspoon granulated sugar
1 teaspoon sticky rice, toasted
and ground to a powder
1 finely-chopped shallot
1 tablespoon coriander
1 tablespoon Thai chives

Method

Prepare the marinade by mixing all the relevant
ingredients. Leave the sirloin steaks to soak in the
marinade for a minimum of 5 hours.
Prepare the sauce: mix the spicy shrimp paste with
the lime juice, fish sauce and granulated sugar.
Just before serving, cook the sirlon steaks in a sear-
ingly hot pan, preferably a cast-iron one (a French
Oven), to your liking (it is especially delicious when
medium).
Next, cut the meat into very fine slices, pour over
the sauce and sprinkle everything with the coriander, chives and shallot. Serve with plain or fried
white rice.

5th District

6th District

49, rue des écoles
75005 Paris
tel : 01.43.54.13.67

BALZAR

Just a stone's throw from the Boulevard Saint-Michel, Balzar has been offering its refined, loyal and enthusiastic clientele a simple and elegant vision of Art Deco for seventy years.

The small café set up by Amédée Balzar - who arrived from Picardy at the turn of the century to serve beer from the cask to students in the Latin Quarter - was taken over in 1931 by Cazes, the successful owner of the *Brasserie Lipp*, an establishment which continues to thrive today, thanks to the "Tout-Saint-Germain-des-Prés" guide.

Cazes once again asked his architect, Madeleine, to modernise and refurbish the café on the rue des Écoles. Since then, there has been a contrast between the beautiful, dark and simple woods on the walls and the mirrors which give the room its sense of depth and its soul. The position of these mirrors, tilted in line with the different slope angles applied to both floors, means that even the most curious of guests can observe - discreetly, of course - the goings-on in the rest of the brasserie...

The menu also remains faithful to the principles of its parent establishment, so much so and so effectively that *Balzar* has, in some circles, been given the surname of *Petit Lipp*. There are no Fargue ceramics, but a young nymph set in a light wooden bas-relief, wearing nothing but a wide smile and carrying two full tankards of beer, offers guests a warm welcome. A Cubist piece which could easily have been created by Braque occupies the left-hand wall, overlapping two mirrors, while a *Champions du Monde* poster can be found at the back in the regulars' corner, setting the scene for the Grasset-published Paul Morand novel.

The select nature of the establishment became evident quickly, distinguishing it as an escape from the hubbub of the brasseries on the Grands Boulevards. Visitors to this establishment have crossed paths with, among others, Sartre and Simone de Beauvoir, together or as individuals, as well as a few eminent academics who ventured out of their Sorbonne lecture theatres at lunchtimes.

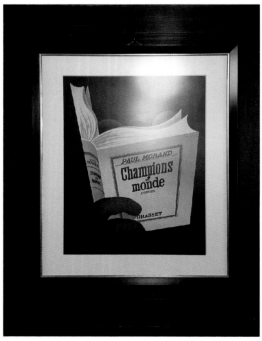

CHOCOLATE PROFITEROLES WITH CHOCOLATE SAUCE

Ingredients

(serves 4)

250 ml milk
100 g butter
200 g flour
10 g salt
20 g sugar
5 eggs
750 ml vanilla ice cream

For the chocolate sauce:
250 ml milk
100 ml cream
250 g cooking chocolate
60 g sugar
25 g butter

Method

Heat the milk with the salt, sugar and butter. Sift the flour. When the milk boils, sprinkle in the flour and mix well using a wooden spatula to dry out the pastry. Tip the pastry into a bowl and mix in the eggs one by one, to obtain a smooth and uniform mixture. Spoon nuggets of choux pastry onto a baking tray lined with greaseproof baking paper, glaze with egg yolk and cook for 20 minutes at 180°C, then leave to cool.

Bring the milk, cream and sugar mixture to the boil, add the pieces of chocolate and mix for 1 minute, then stir in the butter while whisking.

Cut the choux pastries in two and garnish with a scoop of ice-cream. Arrange on a room-temperature plate and pour over the hot chocolate sauce.

3, rue Racine
75006 Paris
tel : 01.44.32.15.60

BOUILLON RACINE

The architect Jean-Marie Bouvier designed this establishment in 1906 (the *Bouillon* on the boulevard du Montparnasse was also under construction at this time) on behalf of Camille Chartier, the king of popular eateries at the beginning of the century. This new establishment offered the local working classes a simple recipe: a single dish of assorted meats in broth, served on marble tables in the tradition of the Bouillons founded by Pierre-Louis Duval.

Clearly inspired by the mass of plant life in the premises, the poet Raoul Ponchon became a regular visitor to this establishment, the second Art Nouveau *Bouillon* to open in the capital. No detail was overlooked: bevelled mirrors were fringed with green almond plants, opaline glass and stained-glass windows were enhanced by irises intertwined with cherry tree branches and wooden panels were delicately carved. From the glazed glass flowers on the front of the building to the mosaics on the floor, from the chairs with their tree-branch backrests to the feet of the bar stools, the décor inside *Bouillon Racine* is entirely dedicated to the world of plants. Master glassworker Louis Trézel created the small molten glass panels

decorated with floral patterns on the ground floor, while Blancard and Laureau put their names to the examples displayed on the mezzanine level.

The restaurant was situated just a few minutes' walk from Saint-Germain-des-Prés, a renowned meeting place for artists and writers at the beginning of the century; its customer base quickly diversified and it became a venue for a number of events. It is rumoured that Simon Vassilievitch Petlioura, a Ukrainian politician exiled in France who was trying to free his country from the grip of the Red Army, may have been assassinated as he left *Bouillon Racine* one evening in 1926.

After changing hands several times, the establishment was finally sold to the Sorbonne in 1956. Transformed into a staff restaurant, this fairytale environment fell into neglect and disrepair. It was not until 1986 that *Bouillon Racine* was able to regain its former glory, thanks to the efforts of the skilled "Compagnons du Devoir" apprenticeship society.

BRAISED LAMB KNUCKLE-JOINT WITH LIQUORICE

Ingredients

(serves 4)

4 lamb knuckle joints
2 large onions
2 cloves garlic
1 tablespoon liquorice paste
or 6 liquorice sticks
300 ml dry white wine
600 g carrots
1 sprig thyme
2 bay leaves
150 g butter
Olive oil
Salt and pepper
Sugar

Method

Brown the knuckle joints on all sides in a casserole dish.
Add the chopped onions and cook until transparent, then add the crushed garlic cloves, the sprig of thyme, the bay leaves and the liquorice. Pour over the dry white wine, then top up with water until the knuckles are completely covered and add a little salt.
Place in an oven preheated to 180°C and leave to cook for 1 and a half7 to 2 hours.
Once cooked, the flesh comes away from the bone readily and is easy to pick up with a fork.
Take out the knuckle joints (separate them from the cooking juices and the aromatic garnish).
Sieve the sauce and reduce it to a glaze, then stir in the butter (100 g).
Adjust the seasoning.

23, rue de Sèvres
75006 Paris
tel : 01.49.54.46.76

BRASSERIE LUTÉTIA

Harmonious reflections of travel, high fashion and champagne grace the many mirrors inside this old brasserie with its post-modern charms.

An elegant figure sits rooted to the spot: hair tied back, eyebrows finely pencilled, make-up perfect. The collar of her black coat hides the lower part of her long face, drawing attention to her sensual, slightly pouted mouth. Locked behind a pane of glass, alone against her small black backdrop, her spellbinding gaze rests on the customers in the room, while a large bubble of white light casts its reflections over her elegant brow. This is just one of the many reflections produced by several fashion advertisements decorating the walls of the premises.

Le Touquet, Deauville, Paris: colourful old posters also offer an old-fashioned ride through this elegant Normandy of the 1930s and 1940s, where Jacques Fath, the young Dior and Schiaparelli would dress the incredibly sophisticated women who strolled casually along the beaches.

Yet we must imagine a completely different place, such as the one envisaged by the founders of the hotel in 1910. It did indeed begin as a luxury destination, and certainly was a place in which to seek comfort, but meat - grilled meat in particular - was the priority here. Nothing could be more normal for a rotisserie restaurant! Free-range chickens, quails, pigeons and in-season game were cooked over glowing embers kept hot by the young kitchen hands. This was a place for telling stories and drinking, while enjoying the grand veneur sauce and flavoursome Burgundy wines.

Slight homesickness and the need to respond to new customer demands drove the owners of the hotel to re-design the premises and rethink its formula, turning it into a brasserie. The interior designer Slavik led the operation alongside Sonia Rykiel (who would later take over the elegant restaurant next door to the brasserie, named *Paris*); the layout we admire today is the result of their hard work. Since then, poultry and game have been replaced by seafood: a blue aquarium now sits alongside the large square bar to prove it.

PRET A PORTER FEMININ

RABBIT FILLET WITH SAVORY

served with bean and streaky bacon stew

Ingredients

(serves 6)

6 good-quality saddles of rabbit
100 g slighty salted butter
1 bunch savory
250 g dandelions
Freshly ground pepper
Accompaniment: 1 bunch spring
onions
120 g streaky bacon
1.5 kg beans
Butter: 100 g
1 large bunch topped carrots
Fleur de sel (Brittany salt)

Method

Prepare the accompaniment: peel the vegetables, set the fattest topped carrots aside for stuffing later and cut the others into straws. Boil the beans and remove their white skins. Chop the onions. Dice the streaky bacon so that the pieces are the same size as the beans. Sweat these pieces in the butter, add the onions and carrots and cook gently, add the beans at the end of the cooking process, together with some rabbit stock and a few savory leaves, then finish with a little butter. Cook the carrots, covered, with a little water, salt and a knob of butter. Clean the dandelions.

Prepare the rabbit: Remove the fillets and use the remaining pieces to make a stock: brown the carcass in butter, add cold water until it fills the pan and cook gently for 20 minutes. Add a pinch of salt. Season the fillets and roast them in the butter, keeping them pink in the middle.

Add a large knob of butter, the roughly chopped savory, freshly ground pepper and table salt to the stock at the last minute.

Arrange the dish: Stuff the carrots with the beans and lay them on the plate, beside the bouquet of dandelions. Season with a little stock. The two fillets should be placed at the front, then dressed with a few drops of the sauce and some savory leaves.

171, Boulevard du Montparnasse
75006 Paris
tel : 01.40.51.34.50

LA CLOSERIE
DES LILAS

The aroma of a Havana cigar floated into the soft, intimate atmosphere of the bar, while a few notes from the piano gently stirred the poets as they dozed at their table. That Tuesday in 1905, Paul Fort, with André Salmon, Rimbaud, Verlaine, and Francis Jammes in attendance, held a literary meeting for the magazine *Vers et Prose* at the *Closerie des Lilas*. This establishment, with origins stretching back to 1847, has been a meeting place for many poets, writers and intellectuals from the Left Bank since the beginning of the XX century.

That year Bullier, an old waiter from the neighbouring dance hall *La Grande Chaumière*, bought the rustic hall on the other side of boulevard du Montparnasse, transforming the space into a sumptuous palatial hall with the added attraction of a park featuring decorative flowerbeds and fountains. A one thousand-foot lilac plantation was the inspiration behind the new name of this *Bal de Montparnasse* frequented by Clémentine Pomponnette and Pauline la Folle, until it was renamed *Le Jardin Bullier*, and later *Le Bal Bullier*. The owner of a small café on the other side of the street one day decided to transform his establishment by naming it the *Closerie des Lilas*. The customers of the *Bullier* quickly transferred their loyalties to this bar, designed to resemble the bow of a ship, and its terrace area, a real little garden sheltered by a tunnel which promised many romantic encounters. In 1925, the establishment was modernised under the direction of the interior designers Alphonse Louis and Paul Solvet. The outdoor canopies became long wood-encased Art Deco terraces, while engraved or enamel-enhanced glass panels were used to increase privacy within this mahogany-clad space.

"La Closerie", as it was called by the regulars, became a central point in the lives of the "Montparnos" and was the setting for many a memorable event. For example, in 1925 a row escalated between Rachilde, a female literary figure, and the Surrealists. She had just published an anti-German text in *Paris Soir*, which upset Robert Desnos and Michel Leiris as they considered this to be an insult to their friend Max Ernst. The atmosphere became more and more intense and blows were exchanged; only the arrival of the police put an end to the situation.

This was Ernest Hemingway's preferred refuge immediately following the Second World War. The writer taught the owner of the premises how to make his favourite cocktail, the white rum, lime and sugar-based daïquiri, which subsequently became a house speciality. Picasso, Picabia, Derain and even Fernand Léger spent many hours there, sitting on the red moleskin seats and setting the world to rights, as proved by the dining suite clearly displaying their signatures in the brasserie. Gainsbourg spent the "first few hours of 1960" in the slightly decadent setting of *La Closerie*, which the singer Etienne Daho called his "favourite place in Paris". Taken over by the Siljegovic couple in 1995, this elegant space, which is saturated with the air of Montparnasse living, is still frequented by a horde of celebrities.

CLOSERIE TARTARE

Ingredients

(serves 1)

165 g minced meat (rump tail steak)
10 g capers
10 g chopped onion
5 g chopped parsley
1 egg yolk
1 tablespoon oil
1/2 tablespoon mustard
1/2 ablespoon ketchup
Worcestershire sauce
Tabasco
Salt and pepper

Method

Mix the mustard and egg yolk with the oil in a salad bowl, as if you were making a mayonnaise.
Add the capers, onions, parsley, ketchup, Worcestershire sauce, tabasco, salt and pepper, then mash together and knead well.
Add the meat and mix well again.
Adjust the seasoning.
Serve with a salad or fries.

6, Place Saint-Germain-des-Prés
75006 Paris
tel : 01.45.48.55.25

LES
DEUX MAGOTS

When Delacroix, Ingres, Balzac and Georges Sand moved into Saint-Germain-des-Prés, a drapery shop called *Les Deux Magots* on the corner of rue de Seine and rue de Buci was selling the fabrics and silks which were so fashionable in Paris at that time. The literary inspiration behind this name, a theatrical play by Michel Sevrin called *Les deux magots de la Chine*, was almost prophetic for this café, which would later become one of the great literary meeting places in the capital.

The successful establishment expanded and in 1873 moved opposite the church in place Saint-Germain-des-Prés, before making way - less than fifteen years later - for a liqueur cafe of the same name, often frequented by Verlaine, Rimbaud and Mallarmé. The current owners' grandfather bought the premises at the beginning of the Second World War and completely redecorated it. The room has fully retained its *fin de siècle* elegance: its furniture with patinated wood panelling is enhanced by the garnet-coloured moleskin of the seats, and its coffered ceiling is decorated with copper ceiling lights. Huge rectangular mirrors are framed by cream-coloured columns decorated with bows and topped with large stucco banners engraved with foliage, flowers and birds. Each of the two magots sits on one side of the large square pillar in the middle of the room. These beautiful multicoloured statues of the Chinese traders, remnants of the original boutique, display a slightly disillusioned expression as they watch the visitors seated at their tables.

Léon-Paul Fargues, in *Le Piéton de Paris*, described *Les Deux Magots* and the other cafés in this artistic area of the city as "true institutions, which are just as famous as state-run organisations". From the beginning of the century to the start of the Second World War, Alfred Jarry and Oscar Wilde, André Breton and his friends, Saint-Exupéry, Éluard, James Joyce, Gide and Elsa Triolet, or even Picasso and the Prévert brothers would meet on the terrace.

The Deux Magots literary prize was created on the day André Malraux received the Goncourt prize for his novel, *La Condition Humaine (Man's Fate)*. While having a drink on the terrace, Martine, a librarian at the École des Beaux Arts, and Roger Vitrac, author of the play *Les Enfants au Pouvoir*, decided to select a thirteen-man jury from amongst their friends. Each member of the jury was asked to donate one hundred francs to a prize fund, which would then be awarded to a promising young writer. The first prize was awarded to Raymond Queneau for *Le Chiendent (The Bark Tree)*.

The premises was one of the rare places to meet and debate in the capital during its occupation in the Second World War: Jean-Paul Sartre and Simone de Beauvoir would sit at their favourite tables near the stove. Political figures, famous singers, painters and photographers have continued to frequent this legendary establishment ever since. It is probably one of the only places where the tourists who visited twenty years ago would still be able to recognise the waiter who served them!

BITTER CHOCOLATE TART

Ingredients

(serves 4)

For the pastry:
130 g butter
250 g flour
120 g icing sugar
Pinch of salt
1 egg
1 vanilla pod

For the topping:
500 g chocolate
250 g crème fraîche
400 ml milk
2 eggs

Method

In a large bowl, mix 1/3 of the flour with the finely diced butter. Add the eggs, salt, the seeds from the vanilla pod and the icing sugar. Mix well. Mix in the rest of the flour. Work the pastry in the palm of your hand. Shape it into a ball, roll it out onto a sheet of baking paper and leave it in the refrigerator for approximately 20 minutes. After taking it out, leave it to rest at room temperature.

Lay the pastry over your tart mould and press it into shape. Bake the pastry on its own for 10 minutes at 180°C. When you have taken it out of the oven, cut off any excess pastry around the edges of the mould.

Cut the chocolate into small pieces, heat the cream and milk and pour the mixture over the chocolate. Mix well. When the chocolate has melted, leave it to cool before mixing in the eggs. Mix without whipping, so that no air is incorporated into the mixture. Lower the oven temperature to 150°C and bake for 22 minutes. Leave to cool.

51, Quai des Grands Augustins
75006 Paris
tel : 01.43.26.68.04

LAPÉROUSE

Diamond grating on mirror was a familiar sound at *Lapérouse* during the Belle Époque when, in the small rooms on the first floor, elegant ladies would assess the value of the gifts they had received from their suitors. The traces left by these jewels can still be seen today, in this quiet and intimate venue. Founded in 1766, the restaurant has always evolved to reflect various changes in the local area.

In the middle of the XVIII century, Lefèvre, a supplier of refreshments to Louis XVI, bought this unusual hotel by the Seine from Forget, who at that time was Maître des Eaux and Forêts (a type of ranger serving the King). The marché de la Vallée replaced the Augustinian convent. Lefèvre then transformed the premises into *Marchand de Vins*: poultry and fine bottles were sampled on the ground floor, while the old servant quarters on the first floor were used by traders and their best customers, so they could complete their transactions away from prying eyes and thieves.

In 1870, the construction of the Halles Baltard - replacing the market on exactly the same site - threatened the very existence of the establishment. However, the literary "Tout Paris" guide discovered the *Marchand de Vins*, and Guy de Maupassant, Emile Zola, Alexandre Dumas, Victor Hugo and later Colette quickly became regulars in the restaurant - which

had been renamed *Lapérouse* several years before, in memory of the seafarer. The Nadar brothers immortalised these illustrious customers in photographs, which were then used to decorate the walls.

At the end of the XIX century, the owner adapted his establishment to suit his new clientele. The walls were covered in Cordoba leather details, while the furniture began to display Empire features. Warmth and mystery invaded the space through the interplay between low, soft lamps; these features were also subtly reflected in the red velvet sofas. The spaces previously used for sales negotiations on the first floor made way for charming alcoves. Wrought furniture in black and chestnut-coloured wood, exotic flowers, model boats and the colonial style of the ground floor bar all called to mind the expeditions of the sailor.

The small rooms became witnesses to all kinds of meetings: lovers' trysts in the "love" room, under the benevolent gaze of the cherubs painted on the walls, or political conventions in the largest "senators" room. The décor and intimacy of the premises has not changed since then. Neither, in fact, has the fame of its customers: Maurice Schuman and General de Gaulle used to lunch there together. Even François Mitterrand used to visit the "flowered embankment" room regularly.

LAPÉROUSE TRADITIONAL PRALINE SOUFFLÉ

with aged rum flavoured caramel

Ingredients

(serves 4)

For the soufflé:
240 g confectioner's
custard (see below)
120 g praline (failing
this, use Nutella hazel-
nut spread)
250 g egg whites
(8 eggs)
80 g sugar

For the caramel:
100 g sugar
180 g single cream
50 ml aged dark rum

For the confectioner's
custard:
250 ml milk
2 egg yolks
60 g sugar
35 g flour

Method

Prepare the caramel: cook the sugar in a saucepan, with
no water added, until it turns a golden, slightly dark
colour. Next, pour the cream into the pan carefully, little
by little, avoiding the small, burning hot bubbles as they
pop.
Pour the rum into the caramel, then set aside.
Prepare the confectioner's custard: whisk the egg yolks
with the sugar, until the mixture turns slightly white.
Bring the milk to the boil. Stir the flour into the egg yolk
and sugar mixture. Pour the hot liquid over this mixture,
then pour it all back into the saucepan. Cook while whisking continuously until the mixture boils, then set aside
in a cool place.
Make the soufflé: grease the 4 soufflé moulds using the
butter and coat in light brown sugar. Whip the confectioner's custard together with the praline (or the Nutella, if
using).
Whip the egg whites into peaks, then add the sugar at the
very last minute, tossing it into the mixer tub. Let the
machine run for 1 minute, then switch it off.
Stir some of the egg whites into the custard, then stir in
the remainder carefully using a flexible spatula, so that
the mixture is not broken up too much.
Fill the moulds, then smooth over with a spatula.
Cook for approximately 12 minutes in a hot oven (200°C,
thermostat 8).
Immediately before serving, make a well in the centre of
the soufflé and pour in the desired amount of warm caramel.

59, Boulevard du Montparnasse
75006 Paris
tel : 01.45.49.19.00

MONTPARNASSE 1900

Simple cuisine set in stunning and elegant décor: this was the Chartier family's recipe for success at the beginning of the century. Bought in 1903, the restaurant at number 59, boulevard du Montparnasse became one of the many *Boullions Chartier* which experienced continuous success. Its features included floral and plant-inspired motifs and finely worked rippling wood; after three years' work, travellers seated at tables inside *Le Bistrot de la Gare* were finally able to appreciate the precision and finesse of its beautiful Art Nouveau décor.

On the wall, a ceramic balustrade topped a bevelled mirror framed by feminine contours in brown wood, while mulberry and bindweed branches stretched all the way along a blue trellis which encircled the mirrors. As they waited for their trains, businessmen and artists would crowd in to revisit their own little Normandy, abandoning themselves to romanticism in this pastoral space. Small, rustic paintings on molten glass at the base of the Louis

Trézel beams provide, among other things, a charming opportunity to daydream and escape from the daily grind. Piercing the immense floral glass roof structure, rays of sunlight would flood the bays in the second room. Scantily-clothed bronze peasants sat on a mahogany railing, proudly supporting glass lamp domes and sensual, graceful lights in the form of tulips.

Taken over by Rougeot in the immediate aftermath of the First Word War, *Le Bistrot de la Gare* became famous and continued to welcome travellers leaving the area throughout the XX century. The interior designer Slavik, careful to respect the original style of the space, renovated the glass roof structures in 1977. As a nod to the history of the *Montparnasse* district, the most recent owners of the premises renamed it *Montparnasse 1900*. Since then, the restaurant has rekindled its early loves, offering traditional French cuisine against a backdrop of marvellously preserved early XX century décor.

SPARE RIBS WITH AUBERGINES
AND PRESERVED TOMATOES

Ingredients

(serves 8)

3 kg spare ribs
1 clove garlic
1 onion
1 sprig rosemary
4 small aubergines
500 ml virgin olive oil
12 large potatoes
300 g preserved tomatoes
4 spring onions
4 tablespoons chopped parsley
100 ml balsamic vinegar
2 tablespoons Worcestershire
sauce
Esplette chilli
Salt, freshly ground pepper

Method

Marinate the ribs and aubergines (washed and cut in two lengthways) with the crushed garlic, chopped onion, rosemary, salt, pepper, 3 pinches of Esplette chilli and 300 ml olive oil and leave overnight.

An hour and a half before you wish to serve the dish, wash and dry the potatoes and wrap them in aluminium foil. Bake in the oven at 180ºC for an hour and a half.

Meanwhile, prepare the sauce: cut the tomatoes into strips, chop the spring onions and put everything in a large bowl, along with the parsley. Season, add the balsamic vinegar, the Worcestershire sauce and the remaining olive oil. Leave the mixture in the refrigerator for at least one hour.

30 minutes before dining, light the barbecue or the grill and cook the aubergines and ribs for approximately 30 minutes. Garnish with the preserved tomato sauce.

45, boulevard Raspail
75006 Paris
tel : 01.49.54.46.90

LE PARIS

A cruise liner with cabins containing several modern pieces of art can be found in the very heart of Paris...

Le Paris is located on the ground floor of *Hôtel Lutétia*, one of the most impressive Art Deco buildings in the capital, designed by architects Louis Boileau, Henri Tauzin and sculptor Léon Binet between 1907 and 1911. Even today, it transports fine food connoisseurs and enthusiasts back to the stylish luxury of the 1930s.

It started out as an elegant tearoom and highly-regarded patisserie, frequented as often by hotel guests (rich Europeans and members of the countryside bourgeoisie) as by the dense crowd of Parisians flocking to *Bon Marché*, the enormous department store sitting proudly opposite the *Lutétia*. Macaroons, opera cakes, cream slices, éclairs and financier pastries were savoured as an accompaniment to rich exotic smoked teas. Josephine Baker came to munch a few madeleines in the company of her many lovers and children, while André Gide impassively scribbled in his notebook there.

The hotel then abandoned its patisserie as so many others had done - a sign of the times - and in 1985 opened a restaurant aimed at its smartest clientele. Remaining true to the building and its "living museum" tradition, the owner asked designer Sonia Rykiel to recreate the atmosphere of a 1930s cruise liner lounge area, which would then be enhanced with a few contemporary works of art.

Beautiful Art Deco wood panelling worked into a precious wood frame has decorated the walls ever since, while the central motif - the silhouette of a bowl overflowing with grapes, pears and bananas - subtly awakens customers' appetites. Several lamps, featuring pure geometric shapes bordered by subtle black lines, cast their light over a collection of contemporary sculptures by Hiquily. A gilded bronze African princess with an intense blue gaze invites you to sit and enjoy the cuisine produced by Michelin-starred chef Philippe Renard, while another more enigmatic sculpture, whose shape is clearly influenced by the sensual curves devised by Henry Moore, sees you out as you leave the premises.

ROASTED SARAWAK PEPPER DUCKLING FILLETS

and caramelised turnips flavoured with lime

Ingredients

(serves 10)

10 free-range duckling fillets,
each weighing 180 g
Sarawak pepper
Fleur de sel (Brittany salt)
10 bunches purple turnips
5 limes
1.5 l chicken stock
500 g rocket
25 g caster sugar

Method

Prepare the fillets: season the duckling and score the skin to form a lattice pattern. Fry the skin side gently, then turn when it has browned. Cook for approximately 10 to 15 minutes, deglaze the frying pan with a third of the chicken stock and leave to reduce by a third, then set aside the cooking juices. Prepare the accompaniment: peel, wash and quarter the purple turnips. Place them in a sauté pan with a knob of butter, the caster sugar and the remaining chicken stock. Cook, covered, for around 10 minutes. Remove the cover and let the stock reduce, turning the turnips regularly in order to caramelise them.

Peel the limes so that none of the pith remains, split into segments and add them to the turnips.

Adjust the seasoning.

Assemble a small rocket salad and dress it with some of the cooking juices, the fleur de sel, pepper and olive oil. Place the turnips in the centre of the plate, then spoon a little sauce over the fillets.

41, rue Monsieur-le-Prince
75006 Paris
tel : 01.43.26.95.34

POLIDOR

Celery rémoulade, liver pâté and blanquette of veal: the menu at Polidor has not changed since 1930. Nor, in fact, has its customer base: "I first ate in your restaurant more than half a century ago", "I have been protected by saint Polidor since 1927" and other glowing recommendations fill the pages in the visitors' book of this inexpensive restaurant in the Latin Quarter. These are echoed in the personal diary of Paul Léautaud, when under the 21st November 1941 he wrote, "Lunch with Marie Dormoy in an excellent restaurant: Polidor, on rue Monsieur le Prince. I think we will continue to go there".

The golden letters spelling out "Crémerie Restaurant" have always adorned the front of the premises. Until the end of the XIX century, the establishment sold butter, eggs and cheese to ladies living in the area. It became a proper restaurant in 1890, when impoverished students from the Sorbonne began to flock there, while Maurice Barrès, Louis Ménard, Jean Jaurès, and even Verlaine and Rimbaud had their napkin rings organised neatly in a small black wood cabinet at the back of this large room with cream walls. A short while later, Ernest Hemingway, André Gide, Paul Valéry and even James Joyce did exactly the same thing.

Squashed in along wooden tables covered with red checked cloths, the "Pataphysicists" made the establishment - a true temple for Hachis Parmentier (similar to cottage pie) and the traditional cuisine of our grandmothers - their headquarters as of 1948. Coming from avid believers in "the science of exception and imaginary solutions", this choice appears truly amazing. Nevertheless, it marked the beginning of a long association: Boris Vian was promoted to the rank of "Satrape" (a leader-type role) in 1953, and the establishment still hosts occasional meetings between the happy bunch today.

Monsieur and Madame Bony, who had been running the restaurant since 1930, decided to sell up forty years later. There was no question of making way for "the pig swill industry", as Madame Bony called it: a law student, who was a regular customer and anxious to preserve the spirit of the premises, took the reins. Offering traditional service and no-frills cuisine, none of the various owners ever compromised the philosophy of the establishment in any way. Although it is still frequented by a good number of students, the establishment is now also a meeting place for tourists who are searching for the Paris of days gone by.

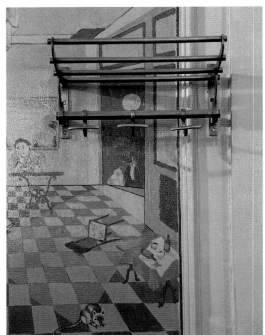

POLIDOR BLANQUETTE OF VEAL

Ingredients

(serves 6)

1.4 kg boned shoulder of veal
4 large onions
2 cloves garlic
1 bouquet garni
1 stick celery
1 leek, white part only
80 g butter
80 g flour
250 ml crème fraîche
300 g button mushrooms
150 g baby onions
1 lemon
300 g Creole rice
100 g butter

Method

Place the meat in cold water to blanch, bring to the boil for 2 minutes, cool using cold water and drain in a colander.

Chop the onions, carrots, celery and the white part of the leek. Place the meat and the abovementioned vegetables, the garlic and the bouquet garni in the oven, on a medium heat, for approximately one hour.

Prepare the sauce "à l'ancienne": peel, wash and glaze the baby onions, then strip the outer layer off the mushrooms and slice them thinly.

Cook the rice.

Prepare the white roux (flour and butter) and mix it into the sauce "à l'ancienne" and crème fraîche. Cook for a few minutes.

Pour the sauce over the meat and serve very hot.

142, Boulevard Saint-Germain
75006 Paris
tel : 01.43.26.68.18

VAGENENDE

The very thought that this little Art Nouveau jewel could have been replaced by a supermarket in 1966 sends shivers down the spine. It was the support of André Malraux, then the Minister of Culture, which saved the establishment in the nick of time.

In 1905, Edouard and Camille Chartier, the founders of a rapidly-expanding chain of Bouillons (establishments which originally served people working in les Halles with a single dish of meat in broth), found themselves enchanted by a small patisserie (and perhaps its location, less than one hundred metres from place Saint-Germain-des-Prés).

They bought the establishment and its internal courtyard, transforming it into a more upmarket version of a traditional Bouillon, on a level with its competitors on rue Faubourg-Saint-Denis (*Julien*), rue Racine (*Bouillon Chartier*) and boulevard du Montparnasse (now called *Montparnasse 1900*).

Construction was supervised by architect Jean-Marie Bouvier who, full of the excitement of "1900", asked the artist Pivain to create a huge collection of paintings on molten glass. These were used to decorate the lower part of the countless bevelled mirrors which created infinite reflections inside the restaurant. Thirty-six little scenes with a certain romantic appeal enhanced this vibrant atmosphere subtly featuring a stone windmill, a calm fisherman and a small town with quiet charm.

The rest of the décor met the criteria and exuberant nature of Art Nouveau style: wood panel tracery, all curves and arabesques, framed the many mirrors; a long braid featuring multicoloured fruit ran the entire length of the bistro, at the same height as the plates of the customers dining there. A large glass roof with green and yellow floral patterns overlooked the premises, casting a soft light over an old gramophone (this can still be heard groaning softly from time to time).

After a few years of activity, the Bouillon was taken over by Rougeot, a great competitor of the Chartiers, before being sold to the Vagenende family, who gave the premises its current name, in the 1920s. The current owner, who has run the establishment for twenty years already, has been careful not to change the restaurant; the reputation of this Bouillon has been upheld and the culinary emphasis placed on seafood. The classification of the ceiling, the walls and the floors in the Supplementary Inventory of Historical Monuments has brought the venue lasting success.

SOLE MEUNIÈRE

Ingredients

(serves 4)

4 soles, each weighing approximately 300 g
8 tablespoons flour
2 tablespoons groundnut oil
80 g butter
3 lemons
Salt and pepper

Method

Ask your fishmonger to prepare the soles by removing the black skin and scaling the white skin.

Season the soles, then sprinkle lightly with flour. Shake to remove any excess. Heat a tablespoon of oil and a knob of butter in a large frying pan. When it begins to bubble, place two soles in the pan, white skin side down. Leave to cook for 4 minutes over a gentle heat, basting them regularly with the cooking juices.

Gently turn the soles over using a spatula and leave to cook for a further 4 minutes. Remove from the heat and set aside. Cook the other two soles in the same way. Set aside.

Melt the remaining butter until it browns, then add the juice of two lemons. Cut the remaining lemon into quarters.

Lay out the soles, pour over the lemon butter and finish with a lemon quarter.

7th District

8th District

41, rue de Lille
75007 Paris
tel : 01.42.92.03.04

LA MAISON DU TÉLÉGRAPHE

Incredible arches support a high ceiling, while an elegant carpet of ochre, brown and yellow mosaics decorates the floor. Ladies working at the post office at the beginning of the last century were offered accommodation in this large ground floor room in a block of flats on rue de Lille. At that time, the State made it a point of honour to provide lodgings for women, often single and from modest backgrounds, who had come to Paris from the country to work in the Civil Service. In 1905, the architect Bliaut constructed this building in the heart of the ministerial district for this very purpose.

The imprint of "social" architecture can be seen clearly in this building. This style, more restrained than Art Nouveau, was inspired by the Secession movement and the German *Jugendstil* which were popular at the beginning of the century. The curved lines of the furnishings displayed no embellishment or extravagance: creepers entangled with flowers decorated only the very top of the windows, and the dark tones of the mosaics reflected the desire to maintain a sense of austerity in the establishment without creating any hint of sadness. A series of elegant but simple windows surrounded the tall, narrow door leading into the restaurant, while on the inside, a large room lit by wide bay windows looked out over a small landscaped garden.

The magnificent building had been taken over and occupied by a different company for many years when Bernard Marck discovered it in 1985 and instantly knew it would be the perfect place for his future restaurant. François-Joseph Graph, who had just restored *L'Ambroisie,* was entrusted with the task of decorating the room. The pieces of signature Serrurier-Bovi geometric furniture rediscovered their original functions. One of these pieces, which at the beginning of the century was used to store the towels, bedlinen and glasses used by the Civil Service ladies now holds bottles of wine, among other things. The colours in the mosaics were fully restored and a mahogany and walnut bar, chairs, and tables were created in true 1900s style.

Highly regarded on account of its charm and elegance, this historic venue (which outwardly offered no hint of its interior decoration scheme) opened in 1987 and became one of the trendiest restaurants in the capital. After being taken over at the end of the 1990s, it underwent a few small changes: the walls were painted in gold-leaf and new crockery was purchased. The ceiling, in places, now echoes the dark violet of the new seats and brings a warm, intimate atmosphere to the premises, although the spirit instilled by Bliaut at the beginning of the century has been successfully retained.

MOREL RISOTTO WITH ASPARAGUS

Ingredients

(serves 10)

500 g short-grain rice (Arborio)
4 shallots
1 glass white wine
1 l chicken stock
1 kg morels
2 bunches green asparagus
Olive oil

Method

Wash the morels 3 or 4 times and leave to dry. Brown them in a little oil, along with 2 finely-chopped shallots. Pour in the white wine and the chicken stock, cook for approximately 20 minutes, drain (the cooking juices can be used in the risotto) and set aside. Chop 2 shallots and fry in a little olive oil. Add the rice and cook over a high heat for 45 seconds, until the grains appear pearly. Next, pour in the chicken stock ladle by ladle as the rice cooks; this process should take approximately 20 minutes. Meanwhile, cook the green asparagus in salted boiling water for approximately 10 minutes. Cool under iced water and set the tips aside.
Add the morels to the risotto 2 minutes before the end of the cooking process. Garnish each serving with a few asparagus tips. Serve, if desired, with a meat or red wine-based sauce.

20, rue Artois
75008 Paris
tel : 01.43.80.19.66

APICIUS

Almost three years ago, just a few steps from the Champs-Élysées, Jean-Pierre Vigato set down his piano in a stunning location surrounded by a large garden, to mark the opening of his new restaurant.

After spending a few years in the avenue de Villiers in the XVII arrondissement, he fell under the spell of an extraordinary space in the very heart of Paris, and decided to move *Apicius* there. The large ground floor and the gardens surrounding it are part of the Hotel Schneider, which was built by the founder of the Creusot Forge sometime around the year 1850 and modelled on the distinctive Parisian hotels of the XVIII century.

The architect Eric Zeller, who works with Jean-Pierre Vigato on a regular basis, completely redesigned the space in order to create a contemporary restaurant without abandoning the spirit of the XVIII century, which truly breathes life into the premises. A large bar has also been installed in a pillared room, where throngs of cherubs play on the ornate Neo-Rococo painted ceiling overlooking a large chandelier, which lights the room for guests as they enjoy their aperitif.

A corridor, which runs for almost thirty metres along the entire length of the restaurant, was designed to provide access to five different spaces: three adjoining rooms next to the garden and two special rooms. Each room holds part of a collection which includes works of art, furniture and chef accessories: in one of the rooms, mottled second-hand theatre chandeliers cast their light over an old wooden table and plates designed especially for *Apicius* by *Sophie d'E.* In the corridor, stunning chests of drawers with draughtboard tops created by *Ginger Brown* are placed next to pieces inspired by the Vienna Secession, or even a large Paul Roland scene from the Royal Brussels Workshop. The patio overlooks a large garden in which art, as demonstrated by several masterly sculptures, is of equal importance.

In this successful mix born of Classical wisdom, a little Baroque madness and design, the owner of the premises offers his guests elegant cuisine which truly merits the frequent honours it receives from various guidebooks and a regular, loyal clientèle.

OVEN-ROASTED SADDLE OF LAMB

with spiced knuckle joint compote and almonds

Ingredients

(serves 4)

1 saddle of lamb, prepared by a
butcher (600 g)
2 small lamb knuckle joints
20 whole blanched almonds
1 drizzle olive oil
1 bunch basil, leaves removed

Vegetable garnish: 2 white
onions
2 cloves garlic
1 star anise
1 small cinnamon stick
Several black and white
peppercorns
1 small bouquet garni
300 ml water

Method

Brown the lamb knuckle joints in a casserole dish
with the vegetable garnish and spices. Add the
water, cover and cook over a very low heat so that
you are eventually left with a type of lamb compote.
Set this sauce aside.

Meanwhile, season the lamb saddle generously and
roast for 20 minutes at 200°C in a preheated oven,
to keep it pink. Simply leave to rest for 20 minutes
(as long as the total cooking time).

Next, add the whole almonds and reduce the sauce
produced by cooking the lamb knuckle joints, until
it reaches a syrupy consistency.

Add the basil leaves to the sauce a few minutes
before serving. Arrange the garnish.

34, rue du Colisée
75008 Paris
tel : 01.53.93.65.55

LE BŒUF
SUR LE TOIT

This famous establishment on rue du Colisée owes its name to the combination of Brazilian-influenced music by Darius Milhaud, a few words from Jean Cocteau and the costumes of Raoul Dufy.

This little show, which at first almost resembles a farce between friends, was staged in 1920 at the Théâtre des Champs-Elysées. The opening night was a real triumph, and was celebrated by the three companions at the *Le Gaya* bar in rue Duphot. That very night, to mark the occasion and with the full agreement of the owner, Louis Moyes, the bar was renamed the *Boeuf sur le Toit* (The Ox on the Roof).

It was a truly migratory ox, which subsequently moved to rue Boissy-d'Anglas, rue de Penthièvre, then avenue Pierre Ier de Serbie, before finding a permanent home in 1941.

Visitors to this establishment crossed paths with the most famous and fashionable figures in Paris: Jean Cocteau and Milhaud obviously led the dance but alongside them, under the watchful gaze of Christian Dior and Coco Chanel, Fernand Léger would call for a piece of jazz while Francis Poulenc and Erik Satie listened carefully to

the words of Aragon, Breton, Radiguet, Claudel and many others. Further away, in a corner, Picasso, seated with his friends Max Jacob, Picabia and Derain, sketched drawings on the edge of a tablecloth while Gaston Gallimard secretly watched, probably dreaming of putting all these amazing memories into writing. There was a fresh and constant sense of excitement bubbling inside the establishment, a real whirlwind of the culture which defined Paris at that time, naturally played out to the sounds of jazz. The celebrity merry-go-round slowed just a little during the war without ever stopping completely, before gathering pace again, even more beautiful than it was before.

The main room - which resembled an Art Deco dining hall on a cruise liner - sprang back to life, illuminated by colossal black and white lights featuring severe geometrical shapes. The mirrors once again reflected the stream of curious individuals who crowded into the premises to hear a few bars of music. The vestiges of this great age - a piece by Picabia, quickly followed up with a substantial collection of drawings by Cocteau - are displayed in the two main rooms, naturally echoing the sculpture depicting Cocteau's head on an ox, which sits on top of the piano.

MONKFISH BAKED IN NEWBURG SAUCE

Ingredients

(serves 4)

1 kg monkfish fillets (net weight)
2 pike quenelles
100 ml olive oil
400 g button mushrooms
300 g shiitake mushrooms
1 bunch fresh tarragon
400 g puff-pastry
2 eggs
600 ml Newburg sauce
2 shallots
100 ml port
400 ml white wine
20 ml Sauternes wine

Method

Reduce the port and white wine with the shallots, a little tarragon and pepper. Add the Sauternes at the end of the cooking process.

Cut the monkfish into large chunks and brown them quickly in a frying pan containing olive oil, over a high heat.

Chop and sauté the mushrooms.

Divide the monkfish pieces into four individual bowls and add half of each quenelle to each portion, then pour the Newburg sauce over until it half fills each dish and add the mushrooms and a tarragon leaf. Sprinkle with pepper.

Cover each bowl with the puff pastry.

Brush the pastry with egg yolk. Bake in a very hot oven for 20 minutes.

Serve on a hot plate.

8, rue d'Anjou
75008 Paris
tel : 01.40.17.04.77

1728

Six steps, illuminated by the light of two candelabras, can be glimpsed through thick violet velvet drapes. Higher up in the building, a narrow glass door opens onto a timeless scene. Constructed in 1728, this unusual hotel in the rue d'Anjou was a particular favourite of Madame de Pompadour and her courtesans.

The row of high-ceilinged and spacious rooms, the typical Louis XVI and XVIII century style Italian furniture, the wood panelling on the walls and the atmosphere inside the hotel d'Anjou in its prime: these are all features which have remained almost intact, to the point that Lafayette, the famous defender of Paris, the liberator of America and a lodger in the hotel in the early XIX century, seems to reside there even today. A bust of this historical figure rests on a single column at the entrance of the premises.

Miraculously saved from Haussmann's merciless pencil strokes, the establishment was nevertheless familiar with the grandeur and decadence of the hotels of "old" Paris.

It took a nine-month restoration period for this unusual hotel to recover its original character. Jean-François Chuet designed the space himself and decorated it especially for his wife, Yang Lining, who runs the restaurant.

Large rooms with heavy moiré curtains, lit by Murano glass chandeliers, provide space for an art gallery and a music room. Baroque, Classical and Romantic pieces belonging to 1728 or offered by collectors are on permanent display, while the room at the end of the row vibrates to the sound of a harpsichord during enjoyable musical get-togethers.

"Along the silk route... from the west Atlantic coast to the Sea of Japan": this menu title says a great deal about the subtle fusion of Western and Asian dishes devised by chef Gao Lin, who is from Beijing. A collection of teapots and a carved wood Chinese folding screen (a tribute to Yang Lining) add to the Asian flavour which subtly permeates these Louis XVI rooms. Refined décor and low lamps with round, red lampshades add to the mysterious nature of the bar, which was designed especially for tea sampling.

1728 BEEF GRAVLAX

Ingredients

(serves 6)

1.5 kg prepared Charolais or
Salers beef fillet
100 g Muscovado sugar
80 g Maldon Sea Salt
2 crushed star anise
1 large tablespoon grated fresh
ginger
2 cloves finely-chopped garlic
Zest of 1 whole unwaxed lemon
1 crushed bird's-eye chilli
(Cayenne)
200 ml Kikkoman soy sauce
20 ml toasted sesame oil
Sarawak pepper (chez Israël)
Souviou olive oil

Method

Place the sugar, salt, star anise, ginger, garlic, lemon zest, chilli, soy sauce and sesame oil in a 1.5-litre jar. Shake the jar as you would a cocktail shaker. Gently lower the prepared fillet, with no chain muscle or nerves attached, into the jar and place it in the refrigerator, turning the jar every 9 hours over a total period of 36 hours.
Take out the fillet and pat with a clean tea towel.
Heat a few drops of oil in a large pan and brown the fillet quickly on all sides in order to obtain a crust on the surface (the meat will already have been cooked by the marinade). Pat dry and leave to cool.
Serve in generous slices with well-seasoned rocket, a drizzle of Souviou olive oil and a sprinkling of Sarawak pepper.

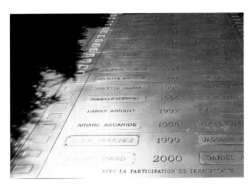

99, Champs-élysées
75008 Paris
tel : 01.40.69.60.50

LE FOUQUET'S

"The national library of elegant Parisian living" is how Léon-Paul Fargues described *Le Fouquet's* in the *Piéton de Paris* publication. A small bar on the corner of avenue Georges V and the Champs-Élysées had been a popular destination in 1899 for the coach drivers of rich families living in the area. Louis Fouquet took over the bar in 1901 and turned it into the leading restaurant on the most beautiful avenue in the world. As a nod to the Anglomania of the time, it was called *Le Fouquet's*.

When Louis Fouquet died, Léopold Mourier expanded and embellished the establishment: the walls of the grill-room were covered in mahogany and "unaccompanied women" were prohibited from entering the American bar; this brought immediate success. Elegant women, such as Liane de Pougy, were surrounded by the likes of Georges Feydeau or Raymond Poincaré.

The Champs-Élysées was modernised after the war: the automobile industry was developing and citizens were discovering the first cinemas. *Le Fouquet's* then became a favourite meeting place for anyone involved in the seventh art: Marcel Pagnol and Marlène Dietrich were regulars, and producers fought over table 22, which had less to do with superstition than the fact that it looked over the back of the Normandie cinema and was a spot from where admissions to the 14.00 showing could be counted.

The establishment, with its ornate banister, crystal chandeliers and heavy curtains, was renovated in 1958, under the leadership of the interior designer Jean Royère. However, the Champs-Élysées was by now less fashionable and the magic of the restaurant faded. Maurice Casanova bought *Le Fouquet's* in 1976 with the intention of relaunching it, and asked his friends from the Left Bank to visit: this included Jean-Paul Sartre, Simone de Beauvoir, Françoise Hardy and Jean-Paul Belmondo.

Two terraces - one on each avenue - were constructed and the evening ceremonies of the Césars (the French equivalent to the Oscars) and the Molières (theatre awards) were celebrated there every year, while José Arthur broadcast his "Pop Club" live from the premises every evening on the *France Inter* channel. The restaurant thus made a triumphant return.

The entrance of *Le Fouquet's* tells you all you need to know about its history. As is the case on Hollywood Boulevard, visitors can see the great names of French cinema engraved on bronze tiles as they walk to the door. The shiny napkin rings used regularly by Alain Delon, Charles Aznavour and Jean d'Ormesson - and bearing their names to prove it - are displayed in the front window three steps further on. Listed in the Inventory of Historical Monuments in 1988, this luxurious shrine to cinema was renovated by Jacques Garcia 1999.

MOLTEN CHOCOLATE CAKE
with almond milk ice cream

Ingredients

(serves 4)

150 g chocolate (51% cocoa)
40 g butter
5 eggs
120 g sugar
80 g flour
1 tub almond milk ice cream

Method

Heat the butter and mix in the chocolate. Add the flour, half the sugar and half the eggs. Thicken the mixture, stirring until it becomes glossy. Mix the rest of the sugar with the remaining eggs.
Mix everything together.
Grease individual aluminium moulds with butter and bake at 200°C for 5 to 6 minutes.
Turn the cakes out onto a plate and serve with an almond milk ice cream quenelle.

3, rue Royale
75008 Paris
tel : 01.42.65.27.94

MAXIM'S

The long feathers of a black and white boa tickled the floor. The elegant Liane de Pougy flirted in the dim light, to the sound of the last few notes played by a gypsy orchestra. The last customers left *Maxim's* and wandered into place de la Concorde as the sun rose over the église de la Madeleine. Singled out by the glittering Parisian youth at the end of the XIX century, this old ice cream parlour became a highly regarded club where the sons of prestigious families would ensure champagne flowed freely as they mingled with escorts until the early morning.

In 1893 the bar was owned by a former waiter, Maxime Gaillard. Anxious to attract a high-end clientele, the new owner - inspired by the English language which was so fashionable in Paris at that time - decided to call his establishment *Maxim's*. When he died, two famous hoteliers, Cornuché and Durand, asked the architect and interior designer Louis Marnez to create a glamorous decoration scheme. Mysterious and luxurious, nature gradually moved into number 2, rue Royale. Copper creepers, flowers and foliage were intertwined across the rounded mirrors, over the doors and around the mahogany pillars. Leaf-shaped appliqués subtly lightened the large room, which was sheltered by a glass roof featuring thousands of flowers, fruits and orange tree leaves. On the walls, delightfully provocative nymphs stimulated deep thoughts in the solitary writers who went there to watch the world go by.

La Belle Otéro and her devastating corsets, Emilienne d'Alençon and Louise Balthy with her English lace parasol - "*Maxim's* beauties" for some and wicked women for others - flanked the American billionaires, Russian barons and members of royalty who attended slightly decadent parties.

Immediately after the Second World War, the magic disappeared. Thanks to Albert, the famous Parisian hotelier, uncompromising on quality and ruthless in his choice of customers, by 1951 the premises had begun to shine and impress once more. Juliette Gréco, Martine Carol, Paul-Émile Victor, and even the musician Georges Van Parys became regular customers.

Already renowned throughout the world for the dining experience it offered, in 1977 *Maxim's* also became famous for its style when Louis Vaudable, the owner at the time, began working with Pierre Cardin. The bar was rebuilt on the first floor and the restaurant, renovated by the interior designer Pierre Pothier, is now listed in the Inventory of Historical Monuments. *Maxim's* has become the restaurant of choice for the Cent club, where a select group of fine food connoisseurs gather. Now more than ever, it is an establishment dominated by, as Henri Calet wrote in *Le Croquant indiscret*, "a distinctive aroma (...) a heady and complex mixture of sauces, alcohol, meat, spices, seafood, tobacco and perfume. Yet only the highest quality foodstuffs are used. It is the scent of pure luxury."

EDWARD VII NOISETTE OF LAMB
with truffeled sauce, foie gras escalopes, artichoke purée quenelles and glazed turnips

Ingredients

(serves 1)

Main dish:
1 loin of lamb with 9
ribs, from which
three noisettes should
be cut
2 large artichokes
40 g fresh foie gras
6 baby turnips
Truffle (weighing a few
grams)

For the artichokes:
1 litre water
1 lemon
1 tablespoon flour

For the turnips:
1 vegetable stock
10 g butter
Pinch of sugar

For the sauce:
1 quantity chicken stock
1 jar tomato concentrate

Method

Prepare the artichoke purée: remove the leaves and the green part, and cook the artichokes in water mixed with flour and lemon juice. Remove the choke, crush the artichokes and mix in a food processor, then pass the mixture through a sieve.

Prepare the turnips: peel the turnips, cook them in the stock mixed with water, a knob of butter and sugar. Make sure the vegetables are just covered and cook until all the liquid has been absorbed.

Prepare the sauce: this used to require a classic meat stock, which takes a long time to make. It is easier to make a chicken stock (Knorr) using very small amounts of water in relation to the quantities indicated on the packaging. Add a little tomato concentrate, reduce and pass through a sieve.

Next, whisk the sauce while adding a little butter and the chopped truffle.

Prepare to serve the dish: once the noisettes of lamb have been cooked - 5 minutes for pink meat, 10 minutes for well done meat - arrange the three pieces of lamb on a plate, placing the purée quenelles and the turnips in between them. Lay the pan-fried foie gras on top and pour over the Périgueux sauce.

115, rue Saint-Lazare
75008 Paris
tel : 01.43.87.50.22

MOLLARD

This is a brasserie which is nearly, but not quite, like all the rest. The building is long and narrow, with wide red canopies and bay windows, and the restaurant specialises in fish and seafood dishes. From the outside it looks like the other, similar establishments in the Saint-Lazare district, but Mollard actually hides an extremely fine and rare example of Art Nouveau décor behind its heavy door.

The story began quite simply: Louis Mollard and his wife left Savoy for Paris in 1867. Despite the fact that neither of them came from the Auvergne, the couple opened a "bougnat" (a small, traditional café which also sold coal) in a small premises which had previously been a popular haunt for postal workers. Madame Mollard served hot drinks from behind the bar, while Monsieur sold wood and coal. Work on the new gare de l'Ouest, as it was called then, was completed and the first department stores opened for business. The area surrounding the station became popular for business meetings, the department stores were attracting a new customer base from Paris and the Mollards made their fortune. Wanting to expand their business, they asked Édouard Niermans, the architect who designed the Hôtel du Palais in Biarritz, the Angelina tearoom and the Casino de Paris, to work on the interior of their new establishment, a brasserie.

A phenomenon of that era, brasseries, which had previously been dark and gloomy, became true architectural delights. The famous architect then transformed Mollard: the walls were decorated with marble and figurative mosaics depicting plant life and fish, while molten glass cabochons were set into a golden base like real jewels. Sarreguemines ceramic panels reflected fragments of early XX century history: the railway links between the Saint-Lazare station and Saint-Germain-en-Laye, Trouville and Ville-d'Avray. Two women in traditional costumes represented Alsace and Lorraine, while a final panel bore witness to the decadent life led by the painter Toulouse-Lautrec, a famous customer of the brasserie.

By a stroke of luck in the history of the premises, the décor has been entirely preserved: immediately following the First World War, the establishment was deserted and the Mollard children decided to cover the walls with mirrors (a very fashionable idea at that time), thereby concealing the mosaics and the ceramic panels. The new owners who took over the establishment in 1929 were totally unaware of the marvels hidden within the brasserie. When he retired in 1963, Émile Saison, who had entered the business as a kitchen hand in 1907 and rose through the ranks to become its director, told his children about the hidden treasure inside Mollard. One beautiful day, a mirror broken by accident ended up revealing the corner of one of the ceramics which had lain forgotten for almost half a century. After ten years of restoration work, the brasserie finally recaptured its Art Nouveau charm. It was listed in the Inventory of Historical Monuments in 1987.

COGNAC-FLAMBÉED KIDNEYS

Ingredients

(serves 4)

800 g veal kidneys
20 g butter
3 tablespoons thick crème fraîche
1/4 bunch flat-leaf parsley
3 tablespoons Cognac
Salt, freshly ground pepper

Method

Prepare the kidneys: cut them into pieces. In a frying pan, heat the butter until it begins to foam, then clarify it by removing the white deposit. Brown the kidneys in the clarified butter for 2 minutes on each side, then set aside and keep warm. Discard the fats released during cooking. Put the kidneys back in the frying pan, add the cognac and flambé them. Next, add the crème fraîche, then scrape the cooking juices away from the pan using a spatula. Leave to cook over a low heat for 2 minutes and season.
Assemble the dish: divide the kidneys between the plates and sprinkle with the (washed and chopped) flat-leaf parsley.

9th District

10th District

12, Boulevard des Capucines
75009 Paris
tel : 01.40.07.36.36

LE CAFÉ DE LA PAIX

A soft, *fin de siècle* elegance dominates this stylish café-restaurant in which gilt, silverware and Empire furniture capture the imagination of all visitors, plunging them into the Paris of Napoléon III.

In 1850, during the lively Haussmann era, the Pereire brothers, the Emperor's favoured financiers, began building a hotel to the north of the old city walls. Its purpose was to host the most elite international travellers as the Universal Exhibition of 1887 drew near. The construction site was presided over by the fashionable architect Alfred Armand, who called on the best sculptors, painters and interior designers to create one of the finest examples of architecture in the second Empire (it would later provide stiff competition for its neighbour, the Opéra Garnier). It was so magnificent that Empress Eugénie, on unveiling the premises, is said to have exclaimed: "It is exactly like being at home; I thought I was at Compiègne or Fontainebleau!".

All the most famous European and American financiers, aristocrats and industry leaders have crowded into this temple of Parisian good taste ever since, to see and be seen. The customers were so elegant that, according to a popular newspaper at the time, "literary types never set foot in the place and tarts feel uncomfortable there".

In 1874, the collapse of the Pereire brothers' business led the Burgundian Arthur Million to take over the establishment, which would remain in his family until 1974. Great chefs such as Escoffier, Ninon and Vignon nurtured the dreams of a clientele which was just as cosmopolitan, but which by now also included artists and literary figures. Émile Zola killed off his character Nana here, Guy de Maupassant visited regularly, and you can just imagine Oscar Wilde watching the crowds go by on the Grands Boulevards.

The *Café de la Paix* takes up a large part of the ground floor of this impressive hotel where show business, royalty and the business world still cross paths.

The coffered ceilings, listed in the Inventory of Historical Monuments, have retained all their brilliance and are enhanced, every so often, with small cherubs which are merrily smoking and drinking.

Large, light-coloured marble pillars punctuate the generously-proportioned spaces in style, while the dark wood of the mahogany and ebony Empire furniture subtly makes its presence felt, plunging the observer into a cocooned atmosphere, far away from the hustle and bustle of the place de l'Opéra.

RED MULLET IN MARROW

with tiny vegetables

Ingredients

(serves 4)

4 good-quality red mullets
200 g marrow, decorticated
200g Chinese artichokes
400 g oyster mushrooms
1/2 bunch parsley
3 sprigs thyme
1/2 clove garlic
500 ml chicken stock
Salt, freshly ground pepper

Method

Ask a fishmonger to fillet the red mullets.
Season, then fry in a little olive oil for 2-3 minutes.
The middle should be semi-cooked but hot. Set aside and keep warm.
Wash the oyster mushrooms and dry thoroughly.
Extract the juices in a frying pan, then add the garlic, butter and parsley. Set aside.
Wash the Chinese artichokes and fry in oil and butter for approximately 15 minutes. Season, then add the thyme leaves and set aside.
Fry the marrow on its own, without any added oil or fat, for approximately 1 minute.
Build the dish: lay the vegetables on the plate and put the red mullet on top. Pour over the reheated chicken stock, followed by the marrow. Season to taste.

25, rue Le Peletier
75009 Paris
tel : 01.47.70.68.68

AU
PETIT RICHE

Le Petit Riche, since its creation in 1854, has attracted only the best customers, from the moderately wealthy to the extremely rich.

While members of the bourgeoisie, political figures and actors lounged on the seats in the *Café Riche* on the Grands Boulevards, coach drivers, machine operators and employees of the Opera house came to seek refuge in this small bistro on rue Le Peletier.

Ravaged by fire in 1873, the bistro rose from its own ashes in 1880, thanks to a new owner from Vouvrillon stock who had a particular fondness for wine. From then on, its multitude of rooms arranged in a row allowed the restaurant to host a more prosperous clientele in a warmer, more welcoming environment.

Since then, businessmen, treasurers, all types of traders, theatre directors and theatregoers have crushed into the establishment to sample bourgeois food washed down with Bourgueil, Anjou, Vouvray or Chinon wine, as recommended by the beautiful golden letters painted on the dark wood at the front of the premises.

As a result of its success, the restaurant expanded to offer an extra forty places in 1920 by taking over the old stables at 19 rue Rossini, which had previously been owned by Monsieur de Rothschild.

The charm of the venue, with its small and large rooms, its crimson velvet sofas, its windows and its subtly engraved mirrors, has remained intact ever since. Even today, the beautiful room at the end with its high ceiling, chandelier, heavy dark red and gold curtains and old paintings and caricaturists' posters, remains the ideal setting for the heated discussions of journalists and politicians.

The bar where latecomers can wait has also retained its painted ceiling, its geometric-patterned tiling and its selection of fine wines.

ANDOUILLE SAUSAGE ROASTED IN VOUVRAY

Ingredients

(serves 4)

4 Andouille sausages
150 ml Vouvray or Chinon
150 ml meat stock
1/4 bunch flat-leaf parsley
75 g butter
Salt and pepper

Method

Pierce the Andouille sausages with a fork so that they do not explode. Heat two knobs of butter in a frying pan and remove the white layer. Seal the sausages for approximately 10 minutes, turning as necessary. Scrape the juices from the bottom of the pan using a spatula.

Place the sausages in an oven dish, add the meat juices, the wine and 1/2 a glass of water, then cook in a preheated oven at 180°C for approximately 25 minutes.

Remove the dish from the oven and set the sausages aside. Collect the cooking juices and stir in the remaining butter bit by bit, whisking the mixture so it becomes frothy. Season.

Assemble the dish by pouring the sauce over the sausages, then sprinkle over the parsley to finish.

7, cour des Petites écuries
75010 Paris
tel 01.47.70.13.59

FLO

Monsieur Floderer fled Alsace only to recreate a better, idyllic, peaceful and opulent version in Paris.

While walking along rue des Petites Écuries in 1909, he fell under the spell of a strange restaurant lost in the midst of the old paving stones: it was an old beer cellar which had been converted into a brasserie called *Hans* in 1901.

The ceilings, wood panelling, copperware, shuttering and stained-glass windows in this chiaroscuro environment were used by Floderer - who renamed his brasserie *Flo* in 1914, his name inspiring nothing but sympathy in those troubled times - to demonstrate his homesickness for an Alsace which had been lost forever.

His fellow countrymen, Hoffman and Sternfeld, created the stained-glass windows, still in place today, providing subtle lighting for the beautiful coffered ceilings and their delicate green and gold frescoes. Floral patterns and architectural elements are intermingled, placing the pleasures of dining in the foreground, while small painted wooden panels depicting parlour games are contrasted

with wooden panelling adorned with animal heads and gilded monsters.

There is a large frieze which runs the entire length of the back wall in the first room; its warm shades create - not without a certain humour - a picture of a lost kingdom where all sorts of dwarves are engaged in brewing and bottling beer. Thundering and vibrant, the little monsters devote themselves, with enjoyment and excess in equal parts, to drinking one of the brasserie's most popular beverages.

The decoration of the second room, which has a more pastoral theme, was left in the hands of the painter Marcel de Tangry, who placed his emphasis on a green Alsace, straight out of a children's story: hills, lakes, rivers and forests are combined to recreate the Alsace which lies on the border between the Black Forest and France.

Erich von Stroheim, and later Alfred Hitchcock - in *A Lady Vanishes* - saw the establishment as the perfect setting for their thrillers, filmed in black and white.

SOLE STUFFED WITH SPINACH

Ingredients

(serves 4)

4 soles, heads cut off, weighing
400 g
20 g butter
10 g shallot
200 ml fish stock
500 g spinach
100 ml white wine
4 puff pastry fleurons
40 ml crème fraîche
1 egg yolk

Method

Braise the soles using the fish stock, 50 ml white wine and the shallots. Set aside and pass the stock through a sieve. Sweat the spinach in a knob of butter for 2 minutes. Prepare your glaze by adding 50 ml white wine and the crème fraîche to the stock in a saucepan and stirring, without bringing to the boil. Stuff the soles and pour over the glaze. Put the dish in the oven with the top heating element switched on and leave to brown.
Serve the soles garnished with a floret.

16, rue du Faubourg Saint-Denis
75010 Paris
tel : 01.47.70.12.06

JULIEN

Four young girls, flowers, stucco work and beautiful wood: this could truly be the formula behind this elegant Art Nouveau brasserie on rue Saint-Denis.

This distinguished branch of Bouillon - which undoubtedly showed up the other establishments in the chain, due to its exceptional splendour and quality - opened in 1904 in a rapidly-expanding district, immediately after Haussmann had begun constructing the Grands Boulevards (almost) next door to *Julien*. Members of the bourgeoisie, traders and curious onlookers crowded in to admire the premises and sample a tasty wine.

The elegance, style and imagination applied to the creation of this universe where honourable muses, animals and plants dominated the entire space, from the mosaics on the floor to the mouldings and glass roof overlooking the room. They almost give today's visitor the impression of being in a gastronomic version of Proust's in *À l'ombre des jeunes filles en fleurs (The Shadow of Young Girls in Flower)*.

Several of the greatest architects and interior designers of that era assisted in the creation of this establishment: while the Cuban mahogany counter, with flowing lines stretching all the way along the bar, is attributed to Louis Majorelle, the masterpiece within this brasserie is actually Louis Trézel's image of the four young women in flower, painted over molten glass and encrusted with cabochon stones and pearls. Very heavily influenced by the Czech Alphonse Mucha, Trézel used the theme of the four seasons when adorning these Graces with flowers and multicoloured stones. The tracery depicting vegetation, lilies, brambles and ivy surrounds and clothes these women, while two peacocks encrusted with bronze stones provide a convincing reflection of their vanity as they circle the vast mirror in the background.

COCO DE PAIMPOL BEAN CAVIAR

Ingredients

(serves 4)

1 kg whole Coco de Paimpol
A.O.C. beans, or 400 g shelled
1 l chicken stock
2 carrots
1 onion
Thyme, bay leaf
1/2 bunch flat-leaf parsley
2 cloves garlic
3 tablespoons sesame oil
Pinch of Cayenne pepper
Juice of 1 lemon
Salt, freshly ground pepper

Method

Shell the Coco de Paimpol beans and cook them in the chicken stock with the carrots, onion, thyme and bay leaf for 30 minutes. Add salt and pepper at the end of the cooking process.

Drain the beans and process them to obtain a purée.

Add the lemon juice and chopped garlic.

Emulsify the mixture using the sesame oil.

Sprinkle with the chopped parsley and a pinch of pepper, then set aside and chill for 2 hours before serving.

Serve the bean caviar with small farmhouse loaf toasts.

38, rue de l'échiquier
75010 Paris
tel : 01.42.46.92.75

LA TABLE DU PAVILLON

It is hard to believe that this venue, behind the elegant Art Nouveau décor nestled on the ground floor of a hotel, was once a hunting lodge owned by King Henry IV.

Nicknamed "Good King Henry" due to his passion for hunting and for women, he had this little lodge constructed at the end of the XVI century. Hunters and elegant ladies met there to enjoy lengthy feasts, sampling pâtés, haunches of venison, rabbit stew, wild boar braised in red wine and roast quail or woodpigeon...

Three centuries later, it was replaced by an elegant brasserie with Art Nouveau accents, where some of the chic and bourgeois customers exhausted by the Grands Boulevards gathered to recuperate.

From then on, lighting in the spacious, curved room has been provided courtesy of a large translucent white glass roof, peppered with floral patterns on which large blue birds perch. The style of the restaurant was inspired by the Art Nouveau movement but shows more restraint, and is calmer than the décor within Boullion establishments such as *Julien* or *Vagenende*, which are positively bubbling over with nature. In an echo of the Viennese *Jugendstil* movement, which the architect probably admired, a truly beautiful room makes up for the absence of traditional stucco and tracery work. The gently curved doors and mahogany panels soften the straight, even room, while the small, delicate mosaics on the floor feature a geometric style heralding the Art Deco movement.

The premises has attracted much attention from filmmakers; for example, Romy Schneider came to shoot a few scenes from *La Banquière* there. For almost half a century, its peaceful and appealing atmosphere has been especially appreciated by a good number of jazz and rock musicians, who go there to unwind after playing a concert at *the New Morning venue*, which is just a few minutes' walk away.

GRILLED SALMON IN BEURRE BLANC SAUCE

Ingredients

(serves 4)

4 salmon steaks
3 shallots
1/2 onion
1/2 clove garlic, minced
100 ml white wine vinegar
200 g butter
1 bunch fresh thyme
2 tablespoons groundnut oil
Salt and pepper

Method

Cut the butter into pieces.
Peel and finely chop the shallots and the onion, then place them in a saucepan and add the white wine. Cook over a very low heat and stir often with a wooden spatula. Leave to simmer for approximately 10 minutes, then add the finely minced garlic.
Now add the butter piece by piece, whisking constantly. Set aside, in a saucepan placed in a bain-marie, over a very low heat.
Sweep the groundnut oil over the steaks, using the sprigs of thyme as a brush. Heat the grill and, when it is very hot, place the salmon underneath it.
Cook for 2-3 minutes each side. Check the fish is cooked; it should be very hot in the middle but should remain pink.
Arrange the steaks on plates and pour over the beurre blanc sauce.

23, rue de Dunkerque
75010 Paris
tel : 01.42.85.05.15

LE TERMINUS NORD

Le Terminus Nord, designed by Hittorf, displays an interesting mix of Art Nouveau and Art Deco styles and provides a beautiful contrast with the Gare du Nord, an enormous monster depositing floods of travellers, tourists and hurried businessmen in the area.

It was originally a café, most probably founded at the beginning of the XIX century, and was transformed into a brasserie in 1870, at a time when massive numbers of people were migrating from Alsace and Lorraine to Paris. The capital then witnessed the creation of quite a few establishments which enabled its inhabitants to explore the gastronomic customs of these exiled people. *Le Terminus*, a transit establishment, offers travellers entertainment and a change of scenery, in a modern and appealing setting. The melody produced by the mechanical piano which still sits in the middle of the brasserie complements the large dance-themed frescoes. Travellers can play billiards or sample the sauerkraut and seafood served in this noisy, bubbly and smoky atmosphere as they wait for the next departure to Brussels or Amsterdam.

The large rooms and straight, even lines of the main room are an unmistakable mark of Art Deco style. The overall impression of the premises is enhanced by geometric-pattern tiling, huge bay windows and mirrors which cover the majority of the walls, bevelling details and the large fresco of the dancers (a theme which is resumed on the lampshades). The ceiling, with its wave-shaped mouldings, is equally amazing and seems to mark a transition towards the Art Nouveau style found in the brasserie.

There is also a stained-glass window featuring curved floral patterns, a perfect illustration of the trademark of the 1900s; further in, a graceful odalisque stretches out daintily along a table. Finally, away from the crowd and prying eyes, at the very back of the premises hides a small and distinctive room suited to more private conversations, in which visitors can appreciate the coloured light filtering through the floral stained-glass windows.

SKATE WITH BEURRE NOISETTE

Ingredients

(serves 4)

2 skate wings, each weighing
500 g
1 quantity court-bouillon
3 tablespoons capers
125 g butter
1 tablespoon wine vinegar
Salt and pepper

Method

Wash the skate under running water to get rid of any stickiness.

Put a large saucepan of salted water on to boil and add the court-bouillon.

When it boils, add the skate wings and simmer gently for approximately 12 minutes. Carefully remove from the heat. Place the skate on a chopping board and remove the skin, then leave in the oven (preheated to 130°C).

Melt the butter in a frying pan, over a medium heat. Let it brown until it is hazelnut-coloured. Take it off the heat and pour it over the skate. Next, add the vinegar to the frying pan for a few seconds, then add this to the skate. Repeat this process with the capers, then sprinkle them over the skate and serve hot, with steamed potatoes.

11th District

12th District

116, avenue Ledru-Rollin
75011 Paris
tel : 01.47.00.34.39

LE BISTROT DU PEINTRE

Crème de cassis, génépi, absinthe: when the *Café de la Palette Bastille* was founded in 1902, its owners were selling homemade liqueurs to local craftsmen. Leaning on the bar, which at that time occupied more than half the space inside the premises, the regulars gathered there from first thing in the morning until last thing at night, under the knowing gaze of the tipsy cherubs painted on the ceiling. These cherubs - gathered in a circle in the clouds - all hold bottles in their hands.

"Tout-Paris", at the beginning of the XX century, turned to the Bastille area for the entertainment provided by its theatres, café-concerts and cabaret acts. Artists and supporters of the arts settled there as soon as the Art Nouveau movement began to develop in the area. At the *Café de la Palette Bastille*, large plant-inspired wooden arabesques created sections in the bevelled window panes at the front of the building. At the back of the bis-tro, the muses of spring and summer, painted in pastel shades on ceramic tiles, cast their spells on seated guests. These Botticelli-inspired women had floor-length hair, gracefully adorned with flowers which attracted the butterflies.

Unfortunately, the ceramic panels evoking autumn and winter did not stand the test of time, but the front structure of the restaurant has been listed in the Inventory of Historical Monuments. In 1987, the Palette found its feet once more, and the establishment was renamed the *Bistrot du Peintre*. Renovation work has not lessened the spirit of the place, and its remaining Art Nouveau features have been restored. The old tin bar, now smaller than its original size, has been restored to its former glory in the purest traditional style, and the regu-lars - artists and journalists among others - now come to sample the wines carefully selected by the new owner.

RAW SARDINE CARPACCIO
with buffalo mozzarella

Ingredients

(serves 4)

8 sardines
200 g buffalo mozzarella

For the marinade:
100 ml olive oil
100 ml lime juice
50 g icing sugar
100 ml wine vinegar
1/2 bunch dill and basil, chopped

For the pesto:
250 ml olive oil, 1 bunch basil
2 cloves garlic
2 shallots
50 g pine nuts

Method

Mix the marinade ingredients in a deep dish.
Fillet the 8 sardines (or ask a fishmonger to do so) and cut each fillet into two pieces. Leave them in the marinade for 48 hours.
Make the pesto by blending all the ingredients together.
Arrange the sardines on a plate, alternating the pieces with thin slices of mozzarella. Place a green salad in the middle, then season with a dash of balsamic vinegar and a slice of lime.
Pour the pesto over the entire dish and sprinkle with Guérande salt.

114, rue Amelot
75011 Paris
tel : 01.43.55.87.35

LE CLOWN BAR

1907. Behind boulevard du Faubourg-du-Temple, which at that time was nicknamed "boulevard du Crime", just a few steps from the Cirque d'Hiver (Winter Circus), a wine merchant's shop closed to make way for a café. That year, at the Palace of the Arabian Nights, electric lamps replaced gas chandeliers while animals and trapeze artists were replaced by cinemas. This extremely popular attraction certainly helped the *Clown Bar* build a regular customer base on top of its existing local clientele.

History does not tell us whether the owner was particularly dedicated to the cause, or whether he simply wanted to make his establishment the most popular in this area, where so many shows competed for customers. In 1919, as soon as Firmin Gémier organised shows at the Cirque d'Hiver which combined athletic events, dancing and singing, the circus - surrounded by Art Nouveau décor - made its first appearance at the *Clown Bar*. Against a yellow, red and green ceramic frieze produced by the Sarreguemines factory, clowns and jesters put on their show for the audience, whose profiles were silhouetted against the wall.

Next door to the Cirque d'Hiver, the *Clown Bar* was a meeting place for famous travelling acts such as the Fratellini, Achille Zavatta or even the Bouglione brothers. The artists from the Cirque du Soleil or the Archaos troupe also visited. Posters stuck to the ceiling in the second room of the establishment pay homage to the shows put on by these renowned artists.

Since the fifth owner of the premises arrived on the scene fifteen years ago, the *Clown Bar* has expanded. Under a starry sky, observed by the clowns created by local sculptor Jean-Marie Pigeon, guests seated in this new space sample Languedoc wines selected with the utmost care by their host.

BAKED BLACK PUDDING

and house mashed potato with crispy apple slices

Ingredients

(serves 4)

600 g Béarnais black pudding
400 g potatoes
80 g butter
1 pinch Esplette chilli
Salt and freshly ground pepper
2 apples (Canasta, Golden
Delicious)

Method

Wash and peel the potatoes, then cover with cold salted water and cook in a large casserole dish. Leave to cook for 20 to 30 minutes, depending on the size of the potatoes.

Drain them and pass them through a mill (or crush with a fork), then add all the butter in small pieces. Add salt and pepper. Set aside.

Remove the black pudding skin and cut it into 5 mm thick slices. Lay the slices at the bottom of four small non-stick moulds and cover with the mashed potato.

Bake in a preheated oven (220°C) for a good 10 minutes.

Turn each mould out onto a plate.

Serve with a few slices of fresh apple (or stewed apple if you prefer).

15, rue Paul Bert
75011 Paris
tel : 01.43.67.68.08

UNICO

Paris has a rich and significant architectural heritage which includes, among other things, the remains of XIX and early XX century businesses: There are still a good number of old butcher's shops, dairy outlets and traditional industrial studios on the ground floor level of buildings dating back to the Haussmann era or the 1900s. In the last twenty years, it has become normal for these repositories of culture to be renovated and transformed into cafés or restaurants.

The creators of *Unico*, an Argentinean restaurant located on rue Paul Bert, adopted a similar approach but one which belonged to a drastically different era. Renouncing the slightly old-fashioned charm of the painted ceilings protected by glass, the wooden shelf units and the Art Nouveau lamps, they decided to set up their establishment in a butcher's shop dating back to the 1970s. Particular emphasis was placed on colour, touches of psychedelia and hints of humour, all infused with a contemporary spirit through a sharp selection of designer furniture.

Established in the early 1970s, just a few minutes' walk from rue du Faubourg Saint-Antoine, the small meat business was decorated in accordance with popular tastes at the time: aluminium geometric shapes adorned the edges of the shop front, which was topped with large orange letters indicating the name and nature of the business, while the inside walls featured chestnut-coloured tiling which complemented the orange lamps.

New owners Marcelo Joulia (an architect) and Enrique Zanoni (a photographer) wanted to keep the retro butcher's shop environment as intact as possible: they therefore left the ceramic features and the façade unchanged, in addition to the refrigerators, blocks and hooks decorating the premises, and added green and yellow vintage-painted paper featuring geometric patterns. Orange, the original colour, spread to the pillars in the restaurant and also formed the basis for the graphics chart used as a starting point for the logo and menu design.

The two business partners finally hunted out a collection of Eames armchairs and benches, a Norman Foster glass table and batch of Scandinavian-inspired armchairs, so their guests could dine in style. In this quirky and joyful atmosphere, guests are able to explore the simple, rich flavours of Argentine cuisine, meat in particular.

CARVED BEEF EMPANADAS

Ingredients

(serves 6)

250 g flour
1/2 teaspoon thyme
1 teaspoon butter
1/4 teaspoon white pepper
1/2 cup milk
1 teaspoon salt
1/2 teaspoon sugar
50 g currants
1 egg yolk
3 tablespoons stock
500 g chopped onions
2 hard-boiled eggs
250 g argentine beef, carved
Olives, if desired
1 teaspoon sweet paprika

Method

Make the dough by forming a well in the flour and pouring the melted butter, milk, sugar and egg yolk into it. Knead the mixture until it is elastic, then roll out the dough thinly and cut out discs measuring approximately 12 cm in diameter. Sweat the chopped onions with the butter in a cooking pot. Add the carved meat and cook over a low heat, stirring gently. Season with the paprika, thyme and white pepper. Add the stock and mix everything together quickly, then remove the pot from the heat. Add the currants and the olives (if using) to the stuffing, then place in the refrigerator for one to two hours. As you are preparing the empanadas, add the hard-boiled eggs, which should have been chopped into small pieces. Place a little stuffing on each one of the dough discs. Dampen the edge of the dough using water, close up the disc so it forms a half-moon shape, and pinch the edges so that they stick together. Use your fingers to pinch gently in order to close the empanadas completely. Fry the empanadas in a mixture of oil and lard, until golden.

1, rue Antoine Vollon
75012 Paris
tel : 01.43.43.06.00

LE SQUARE TROUSSEAU

In rue Antoine Vollon, opposite the Square Trousseau - built on the ruins of the old Children's Hospice, abandoned at the beginning of the XX century - a small "café-brasserie" opened for business in 1907. Artisans and labourers, the traditional inhabitants of the Saint-Antoine area, used to meet there to play billiards, chat and enjoy a drink.

The décor inside the establishment, impervious to the exuberant Art Nouveau movement which was so influential in Paris at that time, was simple but welcoming and the furniture was purely functional. The shop front was created using dark wood and bevelled windows, the cream-coloured walls complemented the classic mouldings adorning the ceiling and wooden tables stood on the floor, which featured a marble mosaic.

Attracted by the "exoticism" of this popular area renowned for its "bad company" and its historical rebellions, numerous stars such as Mistinguett and Jean Gabin came to this neighbourhood café, to slum it in style in the period between the two World Wars.

During the 1950s, the artisans and labourers left their studios to congregate in the cheaper suburbs. This made way for the art galleries, painters, sculptors and musicians flooding into the area, which brought a great deal of new business to *Le Square Trousseau* café before it became a proper restaurant in 1986. The days of billiards and Parisian street urchins were over: the bar, shifted to the smaller part of the restaurant, was reduced by half, while the clientele became chic and bohemian. Singers, film stars, artists and other creative types set up their quarters there.

Although a number of original elements remain (the shop front frame, the wood panels at the bar and the marble floor all date back to that era), the rest of the premises has been renovated. However, this was done with the greatest respect for the early XX century architecture of the premises, to the point that it is almost impossible to distinguish new from old. The peaceful nature of this charming venue and its terrace makes it a favourite filming location for several directors.

ROAST FIGS WITH CHOCOLATE SAUCE AND VANILLA ICE CREAM

Ingredients

(serves 4)

1 bar cooking chocolate
1/2 carton whipping cream
12 figs (3 per person)
Vanilla ice cream
25 g butter
4 ramekins with handles

Method

Preheat the oven to 180ºC.
Meanwhile, melt the chocolate using a bain-marie.
Once it has melted, add the whipping cream.
Make a cut in the figs, slip a knob of butter into the centre of each fruit and roast for 5 minutes.
Cover the bottom of each ramekin with the melted chocolate. Place the figs on top (3 in each ramekin), leaving a space in the middle for a scoop of vanilla ice cream.

Gare de Lyon
75012 Paris
tel : 01.43.43.09.06

LE TRAIN BLEU

"This venue is a museum, but we are not yet aware of this. Future generations will recognise it", said Jean Giraudoux when discussing this establishment. History has proved him right.

Anxious to impress the visitors who would soon be coming from all over Europe for the Universal Exhibition of 1900, the Paris-Lyon-Méditerranée railway company asked architect Marius Toudoire to design the café at the Gare de Lyon.

A masterpiece of Pompier art, the two rooms with their extremely high vaulted ceilings were decorated with exuberant sculptures and gilded stucco mouldings by Édouard Lefèvre and overrun with garlands, foliage, lion heads and nudes. "Mermaids - caryatids straight out of a fantasy world - carry nothing but the dreams of the traveller," said Louise de Vilmorin when describing the paintings (created by thirty different artists, including Allègre, Latouche, Rigolot, and Veyson) depicting the various destinations of trains departing from the Gare de Lyon, such as Antibes, Beaulieu and Hyères. The painted ceilings in the golden room, testament to the bravery of Flameng, Dubufe and Maignan, fused nature and allegory to celebrate the three main towns on the network: Paris, Lyon and Marseille. These paintings, depicting luxurious landscapes where the sky is always clear, the sea blue and the women elegant, invited visitors to travel and to dream, in accordance with the wishes of the railway companies which commissioned the project.

Filled with wonder by such splendour and opulence, Émile Loubet, the Prime Minister at that time, officially opened the establishment on the 7th April 1901. Settled on the okoume and brown leather benches, which would not have looked out of place in a first-class carriage at the beginning of the century, Réjane, Sarah Bernhardt, Edmond Rostand and Colette, later followed by Jean Gabin and even Dali, spent many hours in this unusual venue nestled in the heart of the Gare de Lyon.

It was spared demolition immediately after the Second World War and was used as a warehouse; in 1968 its new owner, Albert Chazal, renovated the premises. Called *Train Bleu* in homage to the famous "Paris-Vintimille" train, the décor within this incredible space was classified a Historical Monument by André Malraux in 1972.

PRESERVED DUCK FOIE GRAS À L'ANCIENNE

Ingredients

(serves 4)

2 lobes foie gras, each weighing
400 g
1 l clarified duck fat
13 g Guérande salt
40 ml Cognac
8 slices farmhouse loaf

Method

Use a knife to remove any nerves and bloody or greenish parts of the liver, then season with the Guérande salt and freshly ground pepper. Add the Cognac and leave in the refrigerator overnight.

To cook the dish: heat the clarified duck fat to 100°C, then let the temperature fall back to 70°C; maintain this temperature throughout the cooking process. Plunge the duck foie gras lobes into the fat and turn occasionally. Leave to cook for 20 minutes. Remove the lobes and place them on a grille to drain. Wrap the foie gras in plastic film and mould it into a cylinder, leave to harden in the refrigerator and then remove the film. Place it in a terrine dish and cover it completely with the clarified fat. Leave in the refrigerator for approximately ten days.

Remove the fat from around the foie gras, then cut it into thick (1 cm) slices. Sprinkle a little Guérande fleur de sel and coarse-ground pepper over these slices. Serve with the toasted farmhouse loaf on the side.

If desired, this dish may be served with an accompaniment of puréed quince or fig.

14th District

15th District

108, Boulevard du Montparnasse
75014 Paris
tel : 01.43.35.25.81

LE DÔME

This is the oldest witness to the lives of the "Montparnos", the artists who brought notoriety to the Montparnasse area until the start of the Second World War.

Le Dôme opened its doors in 1897, after the painters and writers attracted by the Universal Exhibition of 1889 - and the sense of liveliness accompanying them - had deserted Montmartre and resurfaced at the Vavin crossroads, a more popular area in the centre of the capital. Le Dôme, centring around the figures of Apollinaire, Gauguin and Matisse, attracted all the cosmopolitan bohemians of that era: from political exiles Lenin and Trotsky to Bulgarian, Italian or even Spanish artists, many individuals came to experience the pulsating atmosphere of the premises.

Le Dôme was one of the most fashionable places to visit in the city during the roaring twenties. "In those days, many people went to the cafés on the Montparnasse-Raspail crossroads simply to be seen", wrote Ernest Hemingway in A Moveable Feast. The Second World War, however, brought these glory days to an end and plunged

Le Dôme into indifference for several years.
After its renovation in the early 1970s the brasserie, reflecting an Art Deco theme, recaptured its wood-panelled elegance and began to attract a new clientele. The geometrically-designed clock, a witness to the many hours Picasso, Modigliani and even Braque spent in the establishment in times of prosperity, still hangs from the middle of the ceiling. More souvenirs from the twenties, photographs of all the famous customers of the establishment (purchased from collectors Roger-Viollet and Marc Vaux), keep visitors company as they are taken back in time to experience the atmosphere of Montparnasse during the first half of the century.

Since the early 1980s, Le Dôme has been one of the most famous fish restaurants in the capital. A canteen for the neighbouring Albin Michel publishing house, it is also a hideaway for several deputies and senators. François Mitterrand, a great lover of red mullet, went there often. The painter Jean Carzou was also a long-established regular; the fact that he offered the restaurant one of his paintings, which is still on display today, is testament to his appreciation.

TRONÇONS OF TURBOT WITH HOLLANDAISE SAUCE

Ingredients

(serves 4)

350 g tronçon of turbot per
person
Olive oil
Fleur de sel (Brittany salt)

For the hollandaise sauce:
3 fresh eggs
200 g clarified butter
1 lemon
5 tablespoons dry white wine
1 chopped shallot
Cayenne pepper

Method

Cook the chopped shallot, the white wine and the
juice of half the lemon in a heavy-base sauté pan,
until the liquid has evaporated. Leave to cool. Melt
the butter over a low heat.

Place the sauté pan in a bain-marie, add the egg
yolks and mix vigorously using a whisk. Take off the
heat and add the butter little by little, then add salt,
pepper and a pinch of Cayenne pepper to taste.
Sieve the mixture.

Dip the tronçons in olive oil, then sprinkle with the
fleur de sel.

First, cook under the grill, white flesh side up, for
three minutes. Then cook the three remaining sides
for three minutes each.

Pour the hollandaise sauce over the tronçons.

4, rue d'Alleray
75015 Paris
tel : 01.48.42.48.30

JE THÉ...ME

Behind this enigmatic name hides the very simplest declaration of love to the tea which was served here before the premises became a restaurant.

"Desserts, Cognac Dubouché & Cie, Thés, Champagnes, La Françoise Grande Liqueur, Vins fins, Spécialités de Cafés": these old, gilded letters carved into the black marble have lasted an entire century, since a quality grocery store was established on this site in 1904.

At that time, rues de la Convention, de Vaugirard and du Commerce were flooded with small stalls where ladies living locally would meet to chat and buy *delicatessen* goods and other fine foods from the local area and from overseas. Small-scale producers of quality liqueurs, cured pork products and preserves discovered a trusted establishment in their midst, which could act as an outlet outside the *Félix Potin* circuit for the handcrafted goods produced by their families. From then on, the small high-quality wooden shelf units covering the entire room were

well stocked with wines and spirits, teas, coffees, pâtés, preserves and various spices...

The beginnings of mass distribution - perhaps linked to the lack of a suitable successor - saw the end of the small shop, which was replaced in the 1970s by a tearoom. In 1989, its new (and current) owner transformed the establishment into a restaurant while preserving and highlighting the history of the premises, which is listed in the Inventory of Historical Monuments.

The small shelf units and their inscriptions now host an unusual assortment of old tea and coffee containers in porcelain or white earthenware, painstakingly sourced from second-hand shops all over the place. Some animal-themed slipware stands over two Brittany toiles, which are placed next to a substantial and appetizing collection of wines and liqueurs. These drinks can be sampled at the end of a meal and are greatly enjoyed by the political classes, who meet there regularly, irrespective of allegiance.

PAN-FRIED SAINT-JACQUES SCALLOPS

with crunchy vegetables

Ingredients

(serves 4)

800 g Saint-Jacques scallops
Olive oil
20 g butter
1 courgette
1 pepper
2 cabbage leaves
1 aubergine
2 tomatoes
2 leeks
1 onion
Bouquet garni of savory, parsley,
bay leaf, thyme, oregano, celery
Tabasco
Harissa

Method

Mix 2 tablespoons olive oil and 10 g butter in a frying pan and leave to brown. Sear the Saint-Jacques scallops for 30 seconds on each side, then sprinkle over some fleur de sel and Szechuan pepper and set aside at room temperature.

Chop the onion finely and leave to sweat in the pan. Dice all the vegetables apart from the leek. Brown them with the onion already in the pan and leave to cook for half an hour over a medium heat.

At the very last minute, add 5 drops of Tabasco and 1 g harissa.

Create a vegetable mosaic base, place the Saint-Jacques scallops around it and finish with a drizzle of olive oil and some chives.

Serve, if desired, with a chanterelle fricassee.

16th District

17th District

11, place des états-Unis
75016 Paris
tel : 01.40.22.11.10

LA CRISTAL ROOM

A discreet freestone façade in the Place des États-Unis hides a truly special hotel with an exceptional destiny. Taken over by Baccarat in 2003 and completely renovated by Philippe Starck, it is now home to the head office of the prestigious crystal manufacturer as well as a restaurant, the *Cristal Room*, which is located in the old Noailles dining room.

As enchanted by the character of his sponsor as by the memories lingering within the premises, Philippe Starck drew on both unusual stories when stylishly renovating this house in which poetry, aesthetics, cultural heritage and design are marvellously interlinked, breathing life back into this sleeping beauty.

It was built in 1895 by the architect Paul Ernest Sanson, on behalf of Maurice Bischoffsheim, a powerful banker. Almost twenty years later, his daughter Marie-Laure, a symbolic figure in the art world, took over the distinctive hotel with her husband Charles de Noailles, with the aim of making it one of the most highly-regarded function rooms in the capital. The lady of the establishment, whose imagination and inquisitive nature are still legendary, then asked the interior designer Jean-Michel Franck to create an awe-inspiring room using cream-coloured ray skin and straw marquetry décor. In this unusual setting, where pieces by Reubens and Watteau were interspersed with works by Braque, Klee and Picasso, aristocrats, businessmen

and artists mingled during extraordinary parties. Luxury was combined with style and unrestrained imagination, resulting in what some people were quick to label "bizarre aesthetics".

Marie-Laure de Noailles would, without a doubt, have applauded this new universe, for which Philippe Starck had been given carte blanche. The *Cristal Room*, which is accessed via a bright carpet, has retained the imagination and "Baroque spirit" which inhabited the premises in days gone by: the walls, with their ochre bricks encased in golden frames and marble, have been conserved and are now enhanced with medallions. The Baccarat chandeliers, ceiling lights and glasses blend naturally with the contemporary furniture, chairs, sofas and red cushions to create a magnificent overall effect.

A small room with a fleece-lined ceiling, from which sprouts an impressive black chandelier, lies next to the main room, while for certain evening events a large table is set up on the large staircase, in front of an incredible glass library where museum pieces are on display.

It is within this elegant and dreamlike setting that chef Thierry Burlot has developed a subtle and lively cuisine, leading guests a little deeper into the pleasure of the senses...

OYSTER AND CURRANT TARTARE

Ingredients

(serves 4)

12 size 1 oysters
6 baby leeks
1 shallot
1 bunch chives
2 sweet red peppers
1 bunch spring onions
1 bunch currants

For the pastry:
250 g flour
35 ml olive oil
7 g salt
65 ml water
170 g butter
1 bouquet green shiso
1 stick lemongrass

Method

Prepare the pastry, then roll it out between two sheets to a thickness of 2 mm. Cook it between 2 baking sheets. Cut it while hot, into strips 2 cm wide and 15 cm long.

Open and strain the oysters, chop them up and add the leeks, the thin slices of spring onion and the pepper. Finely chop the chives and the shallot.

Make a currant jam.

Spoon the tartare onto the pastry, add a few drops of jam, then arrange a few sticks of lemongrass and the green shiso heads on top.

19, chaussée de la Muette
75016 Paris
tel : 01.42.15.15.31

LA GARE

Like the entire network of stations along the inner ring road, La Gare - the Chaussée de la Muette station - closed its doors in 1981, after a century of offering travellers in the 16th arrondissement an efficient and reliable service.

The fortunes of the premises varied after this, as did the fortunes of most other similar locations. Subsequently used as a florist, a commercial estate agency and a showroom, the old station, peacefully sitting right in the centre of the Chaussée de la Muette, was purchased in 1996 by a restaurateur who fell under the spell of this unusual site.

The quiet red-brick entrance, elegantly topped with a round white clock, still occasionally welcomes the nostalgic "elders" of the area, who come to reminisce about the era when the trains were still running. This welcoming atmosphere provided a refuge for members of the bourgeoisie, working-class individuals and traders alike as they headed for the outskirts of Paris. They would all wait here for the next departure, under the shelter of the vast metal structures supporting the railway building.

Although this procession of customers continues today, the voyage is now a gastronomic one. The ticket offices on the ground floor have been replaced by a comfortable bar surrounded by patent leather club armchairs, an essential stop-off point before descending the huge staircase leading to the platforms.

An old floor with simple, thick floorboards supports the many tables which are flooded with pleasant natural light during the day; at night the lighting is more subdued, subtly surrounding the groups of diners separated by large red velvet curtains.

A collection of videos is projected into the centre of the many mirrors lining the wall and running the entire length of the restaurant. These videos, faithful to the spirit of the premises, evoke movement, travel and nature, so much so that visitors have no difficulty in imagining they are leaving for an unknown destination on a more modern version of the Orient Express.

DELICATE TOMATO AND MOZZARELLA TART
with roast red mullet fillets

Ingredients

(serves 5)

10 rectangular rolled puff pastry
sheets measuring 3x7 cm
6 small, very red tomatoes
100 g mozzarella
1 head of garlic
1 bunch basil
1 bunch spring onions
5 x 250 g red mullet pieces
100 ml olive oil
100 g stoned niçoise olives
100 g capers
2 anchovy fillets

Method

Chop and stew the spring onions to make a jam.
Spread the jam mixture onto the sheets of pastry.
Chop and deseed the tomatoes, preserve with the
garlic, thyme, olive oil, salt and pepper.
Cut the mozzarella into pieces and marinate in olive
oil, basil, salt and pepper.
Build the tarts by spreading on a layer of the preserved tomatoes, followed by a piece of mozzarella and
the basil leaves.
Roast the red mullet fillets in the oven for a few
minutes.
Make a tapenade by mixing the olive oil with the
basil, olives, capers and anchovies.
Assemble the dish by placing the red mullet fillets
alongside the warm tart and adding a little tapenade.

Allée de Longchamp
75016 Paris
tel : 01.45.27.33.51

LA GRANDE CASCADE

Anxious to offer Parisians the chance to enjoy the fresh air, Napoléon III decided to reorganise a large part of the green spaces within the capital. Taking London's Hyde Park, a development he hoped to rival, as a model, the Emperor entrusted the gargantuan task of remodelling the Bois de Boulogne to the engineer and landscaper Jean-Charles Alphand and the architect Gabriel Davioud, under the leadership of Baron Haussmann.

Paths, lakes, islands, wells, ponds and waterfalls have been dotted across the landscape ever since. So that he was able to stop and relax there while out walking, the Emperor ordered a wooden pavilion to be built at the foot of one of these waterfalls, nicknamed the "Grande Cascade" (Large Waterfall) because of its size (it is 10 metres wide and 14 metres high). This pavilion was transformed into a restaurant for the Universal Exhibition of 1900. As it was not far from the Champs-Élysées and very fashionable at the time, the venue became a popular meeting place for stylish Parisians and the setting for many a romantic rendezvous. Due to its proximity to the Longchamp and Auteuil racecourses, it was also a popular haunt for racegoers.

Several café owners and brewers took over *La Grande Cascade* before the premises became an actual restaurant. After its renovation in the late 1980s by the Menut family, which had owned the premises for over forty years, the *Grande Cascade* successfully regained its former glamorous atmosphere: French-style furniture, drapes and soft furnishings were used to decorate the majestic main room.

The Napoleon III ceilings were badly damaged and had to be reconstructed: mouldings, cherubs and flower garlands now line the edges of a large square glass roof, and cloudy skies have been painted onto the ceilings in the rotunda and the adjacent rooms. At the foot of a beautiful staircase leading to the Longchamp room sits a mahogany bar, lit by chandeliers adorned with many pendants, while the rotunda of Napoléon III's luxurious and quiet pavilion opens out onto a shady terrace, overlooked by an impressive canopy which has also been restored.

PAN-FRIED SAINT-JACQUES SCALLOPS

with chicory and beurre noisette, garnished with grated black truffle

Ingredients

(serves 4)

12 Saint-Jacques scallops
20 ml walnut oil
160 g butter
4 portions chicory
50 g butter
Juice of 2 lemons
Pinch of sugar
Salt and pepper
1 truffle weighing 50 g

Method

Open the Saint-Jacques scallops, remove the beards and rinse under running water; leave to dry on a cloth.

Separate the chicory leaves so that they are all the same size, then cut off the ends and wash them.

Cook them, covered, with water, 50 g butter, sugar, salt, pepper and the juice of 1 lemon. Once cooked, cut them lengthways.

Beurre noisette: melt 100 g butter in a saucepan until it begins to brown. Add the juice of 1 lemon, salt and pepper immediately.

To finish the dish: pan fry the Saint-Jacques scallops and chicory.

Dress with the beurre noisette sauce.

Grate a black truffle over the Saint-Jacques scallops.

16, avenue Victor Hugo
75016 Paris
tel : 01.44.17.35.85

PRUNIER

It was in 1904, during his honeymoon in the Norwegian fjords, that restaurateur Émile Prunier discovered fisheries and saw the potential in buying, transporting and selling live fish.

Following in the footsteps of his father Auguste, the founder of one of the most highly-regarded oyster restaurants in Paris, Émile, a trained engineer, was greatly inspired by the scientific advancements made during his lifetime. Having designed a system which made it possible to pump oxygen into large baths of fresh water, then salt water, he was able to transport fresh and live fish to France and later to neighbouring countries. He rapidly established himself as the leading fish specialist in Europe, and Gustave de Suède and Marie de Roumanie began visiting his establishment regularly.

By 1925 Émile Prunier's success was confirmed; he decided to open a new restaurant. Émile, a true art lover and a man of style, wanted to create the most modern and elegant premises in the entire capital. Entranced by the Art Deco style which had slowly but surely established itself in the preceding ten years, he asked architects Boileau and Carrière, sculptor Brodowidz and some of the students taught by Lalique, Le Bourgeois and Labouret to create a building, which was (and still is) the undisputed jewel in the crown of the Parisian Art Deco movement.

While the façade - displaying voluptuously intertwined circles delicately set with geometric patterns - oozes charm, the interior plunges visitors into a true geometric spectacle.

A thousand and one tightly-bunched small triangles rise towards the ceiling like golden fireworks on a black marble background, while gold and white circles interact with small rectangular mosaics as they trace golden swirls on the floor, resembling the curved back of a fish as it leaps out of the water.

Magnificent gilded wood panels still gracefully decorate the bar today and were enhanced a few years ago by a contemporary aquarium, created especially for *Prunier* by the American Bob Wilson.

The incredible staircase leads to a vast room created by the interior designer Jacques Grange, who took his inspiration from ancient Russian legends and tales in order to create a more intimate, dreamlike space.

The plates, re-issues of 1932 Mathurin Méheut creations, capture the attention of customers with their sea-blue shades. True to the founder's tradition, they hold "anything which comes from the sea".

BRETON LOBSTER

with young beetroot shoots, diced papaya and passionfruit

Ingredients

(serves 4)

Main dish:
2 Breton lobsters
2 papayas
1 passion fruit
1 mango
1/2 bunch chervil
1/2 bunch chives
100 g small yellow-skinned potatoes
150 g beetroot shoots
100 g mixed green salad or mixed
young leaves
Table salt, fleur de sel and freshly
ground pepper

For the vinaigrette:
50 ml lobster stock
50 ml balsamic vinegar
50 ml olive oil
100 ml groundnut oil
20 ml hazelnut oil

For the court-bouillon:
2 l water
150 ml vinegar
250 ml white wine
1 stick celery
1 large onion
1 carrot
1 bouquet garni
1 teaspoon coarse salt
1 teaspoon black pepper

Method

Make the court-bouillon:
Wash, peel and chop the carrot, onion and celery. Place the water in a pan and add the vinegar, wine, coarse salt, grains of pepper and the bouquet garni. Bring to the boil, then plunge the lobsters into the pan. When the pan contents come back to the boil, cook for 5 minutes then leave everything to cool, before shelling the lobsters.
Separate the salad leaves and wash, together with the beetroot shoots. Chop the chervil and chives.
Peel, wash and chop the potatoes into 3 mm cubes, then boil for 2 to 3 minutes.
Peel the papaya, cut half into thin strips and the other half into 3 cm cubes.
Scoop out the passion fruit flesh.

Make the vinaigrette then add the diced potato and papaya, the passion fruit flesh and the chives.
Mix the salad and shoots together, then add a few drops of the vinaigrette.
Split the lobsters in two and place half a lobster on each plate. Add the salad, the mango slices and the claws. Finish with the vinaigrette and garnish with the chervil, then season with the fleur de sel and pepper.

10, rue Gustave Flaubert
75017 Paris
tel : 01.42.67.05.81

LE BISTROT D'À CÔTÉ

Butter, eggs and cheese have been replaced by the many coloured tiles which have breathed new life into this old dairy shop and quality grocery store, which dates back to the beginning of the century.

Set up inside number 10, rue Gustave Flaubert, in a prosperous area of des Ternes, Monsieur Roumy's shop - "a trusted establishment" according to the advertisement - sold good quality, fresh products, whole and semi-skimmed milk, clotted cream and all kinds of cheeses.

As was the case with many small businesses at that time, whether specialist pork butchers or bakeries, the decoration was neat and well looked-after. Delicate wood and copper shelf units ran all the way along each wall and held - besides the dairy goods - jams, preserves, poultry terrines, herbs and flavourings, China teas and African coffees, to the great joy of fine food connoisseurs in the area. As customers queued to pay, they would have been able to appreciate two pleasant frescoes with a floral theme overlooking Madame Roumy's till, which was placed on top of a solid wood and white marble sideboard. Yellow and black painted glass lamps, a Muller Frères Lunéville design in the range of Gallé creations and a product of the Nancy school, evoked the mystical, exotic Orient, and bathed the large room in a warm light.

One hundred years later, the premises has not lost any of its charm. The beautiful dark wood at the front of the building has retained its Art Nouveau tracery and its rural pastoral themed scene. Only the fresh products and the *delicatessen* foods have disappeared from the old shelf units, as Michel Rostang, the new owner, has a weakness for old *Michelin* guides and slipware: Henry IV now sits there, beside Napoléon, Joan of Arc and Poincaré.

OMELETTE WITH CEPS AND TRUFFLES

Ingredients

(serves 4)

10 eggs
500 g lamb kidneys
100 g rabbit liver
20 g duck fat
200 g preserved ceps
1/2 bunch flat-leaf parsley
1 clove garlic
Salt and pepper

Method

Prepare the kidneys by removing the fat, the central nerve and the membrane. Dice them. Next, dice the poultry livers.

Wash and chop the parsley, then peel and slice the clove of garlic.

Melt half the duck fat in a frying pan, then brown the kidneys and livers on each side. Season, then add the garlic and half the parsley. Set aside.

Break the eggs into a bowl, then beat them and add the kidneys and livers.

Melt the remaining fat, then pour in the first mixture. Cook for a few minutes over a low heat, then add the drained ceps and the thinly-sliced truffles. Leave to cook for 4 minutes. Set aside.

Garnish by sprinkling the remaining parsley over the omelette.

19th District

20th District

188, avenue Jean Jaurès
75019 Paris
tel 01.42.39.44.44

LE BŒUF COURONNÉ

In Paris, in 1867, butchers and agents in the *Bar du Petit Bœuf* usually negotiated the price of meat over a glass of white wine.

Across the road, just a few minutes' walk from the newly-built Villette slaughterhouse, the cattle market would have been in full swing. The brasserie, which had a rustic-themed décor (checked walls and wooden benches, tables and chairs), was connected to a proper restaurant offering more elaborate cuisine: beef ribs and tender Charolais cuts were served in a vast wood-panelled room to guests sitting on the wide leather seats. Established under Napoléon III, this temple of meat was appropriately named *Le Bœuf Couronné* (The Crowned Ox).

The disappearance of the slaughterhouses in the 1960s sounded the death knell for the last remaining shipping agents doing business on the premises. However, the establishment had acquired a solid reputation amongst lovers of good-quality meat, who never thought twice about making their way across the whole of Paris to dine there.

The old beech wood chopping blocks, remnants of a bygone age and scarred by many knife blades, now sit at the back of the restaurant, while the brasserie still displays a board which in the past was used to inform shopkeepers of the price of meat every day.

The Cité de la Musique has taken the place of the Villette slaughterhouse and the market. Tourists and music lovers crowd into Au *Bœuf Couronné*, which has gained a new lease of life. A keen meat-eater, Jacques Brel has become a regular guest, while various musicians and singers come to dine there after their shows. Making reference to the new activities undertaken in the area, paintings depicting all kinds of musical instruments hang on the walls of the restaurant.

Anyone who enjoys the finer things in life can also make use of the new small room on the first floor, which is totally dedicated to cigar smoking. Comfortably seated in red leather armchairs, Havana enthusiasts round off their evening under the watchful gaze of the most famous cigar smokers in history, who have been immortalised in black and white photographs.

CALF'S HEAD WITH A RAVIGOTE SAUCE

Ingredients

(serves 4)

1 calf's head to serve 4
250 g carrots
celeriac
200 g onion
2 bay leaves
6 allspice berries
1 lemon
100 g flour
60 g capers
6 gherkins
1 small onion
1/2 bunch parsley
Olive oil
Wine vinegar
1 tablespoon mustard

Method

Clean the head and tongue under running water and soak for approximately 6 to 7 hours, then leave to dry. Place them in a large pan, cover with cold water and leave to boil (blanch) for approximately 10 minutes. Cool under running water, dry, then squeeze the juice of half the lemon over the head, to prevent it from discolouring. Split the head into portions.

Prepare the tongue. Mix a little flour and cold water in a sufficiently large pan, then add lemon juice and coarse salt. Add 3 sliced carrots, the celeriac, 2 chopped onions, the 2 bay leaves, 6 allspice berries and then add more water if necessary.

Bring to the boil, stirring frequently. Add the calf's head and the tongue. Cover and leave to cook for approximately 2 to 3 hours. Remove the tongue before the head is ready, as the latter will take longer to finish cooking.

For the ravigote sauce: Mix the capers, the gherkins, the onions and the chopped parsley together, then stir the mixture into a mustard vinaigrette.

1, rue Jourdain
75020 Paris
tel : 01.46.36.65.81

ZÉPHYR

"Tout-Paris" in the roaring Twenties danced to the beat of the foxtrot and the shimmy while cabaret singer Môme Moineau sang in the Belleville area; the Relais des Pyrénées at number 1, rue Jourdain, on the boundary between the 19th and 20th arrondissements, also opened for business. The interplay between mirrors fringed with dark wood, console tables featuring geometric lines, wide sofas and leather chairs, and of course the sophisticated Art Deco atmosphere, attracted the people who came to the Buttes Chaumont area for a stroll as well as the local residents, a mixture of labourers and artists.

Renowned and rewarded for its top quality cuisine, in the immediate aftermath of the Second World War the restaurant became a favourite venue of fine food connoisseurs living in Paris. Famous for its Basque and Béarnaise specialties, lavish dinners would be capped off with an old fruit liqueur, and guests would stretch out many of their evenings as much as possible by gathering around the grand piano which (until recently) sat proudly in the main room.

Taken over in 1989, *Le Relais des Pyrénées* made way for *Zéphyr*. As if to restore the link with the anti-traditional ideas which gave rise to the Art Deco movement, a fresco (inspired by the Cubism of Georges Braque and Juan Gris) featuring jazz scores on newspapers, which in turn are transformed into game tables, was painted at the very top of the restaurant walls.

Wishing to recover a more simple form of conviviality, the new owners pulled down the partition wall which had, up to that point, separated the bar from the restaurant. The premises was taken over again in 2001, and although the plumbing and electrical wiring was modernised for the first time since the restaurant was established (up to that point, the building still had lead pipes and porcelain switches), the wood panelling and most of the furniture remaining in this very old house are the original features.

ROQUEFORT CRÈME BRÛLÉE

Ingredients

(serves 4)

1 litre whipping cream
10 egg yolks
5 g salt
200 g Roquefort

Method

Mix the egg yolks with the (slightly melted) Roquefort.
Add the salt and the liquid cream.
Cook in the oven at 100°C, in a bain-marie, for 30 minutes.
Leave to rest in the refrigerator.
Sprinkle with light brown sugar and caramelise before serving.
Serving suggestion: serve with a Roquefort sorbet on a fresh herb chiffonnade.

Index of the recipes

Fish

Monkfish baked in Newburg sauce 135
Le Bœuf sur le Toit

Monkfish with sweet peppers and tapenade 23
Le Zimmer

Pan-fried Saint-Jacques scallops, 217
with crunchy vegetables
Je Thé...Me

Skate with beurre noisette 183
Le Terminus Nord

Red Mullet in marrow, with tiny vegetables 161
Le Café de la Paix

Grilled salmon in beurre blanc sauce 179
La Table du Pavillon

Sole stuffed with spinach 169
Flo

Sole Meunière 119
Vagenende

Tronçons of turbot with Hollandaise sauce 213
Le Dôme

Vegetables

Jerusalem artichokes a la Darphin 19
Le Grand Véfour

Omelette with ceps and truffles 243
Le Bistrot d'à Côté

Desserts

Rum baba, with ginger and pineapple jam, 55
served with vanilla ice cream
Guillaume

Crêpes Alexandre 37
Gallopin

Roast figs with chocolate sauce 201
and vanilla ice cream
Le Square Trousseau

Peaches in Carpentras lime blossom 69
syrup, with currant sorbet
Le Dôme du Marais

Molten chocolate cake, 145
with almond milk ice cream
Le Fouquet's

Kugelhopf French toast, 65
quetsche plum compote and caramel ice cream
Bofinger

Chocolate profiteroles with chocolate sauce 81
Le Balzar

Lapérouse traditional praline soufflé, 103
with aged rum flavoured caramel
Lapérouse

Bitter chocolate tart 97
Les Deux Magots